1 MONTH OF
FREE
READING

at

www.ForgottenBooks.com

By purchasing this book you are
eligible for one month membership to
ForgottenBooks.com, giving you
unlimited access to our entire
collection of over 1,000,000 titles via
our web site and mobile apps.

To claim your free month visit:

www.forgottenbooks.com/free130526

ISBN 978-1-5283-8080-5
PIBN 10130526

GOD'S RULE

FOR

CHRISTIAN GIVING.

A PRACTICAL ESSAY

ON THE

SCIENCE OF CHRISTIAN ECONOMY.

BY

WILLIAM SPEER,

SECRETARY OF THE PRESBYTERIAN BOARD OF EDUCATION.

———

PHILADELPHIA:
PRESBYTERIAN BOARD OF PUBLICATION,
1334 CHESTNUT STREET.

WESTCOTT & THOMSON,
Stereotypers and Electrotypers, Phila.

PREFACE.

THIS volume is the offspring of practical necessities, connected with the labors of a commission and ordination similar to that which Paul, when the time of his departure was at hand, bestowed upon Timothy: "Watch thou in all things; endure afflictions; do the work of an evangelist; make full proof of thy ministry."

"To do the work of an evangelist," the writer was sent to China in the year 1846. He spent several years there amidst the protracted scenes of that horrible war by which Christian nations, for money, succeeded at length in compelling the government of a great and peaceful heathen empire to legalize a traffic which was deliberately poisoning with opium, year by year, millions of its people.

In the year 1852 he was sent to California to preach Christ to the Chinese whom the power of money brought there, amidst the tens of thousands from all the nations of the habitable globe. He witnessed the strange, frantic intoxication of those multitudes; and saw the crimes which men were willing to commit for money. In 1857 he was obliged to leave his work, exhausted and expected to die, partly because, amidst the boundless and most important work to be done in that field, the Christians of our country enabled the Board of Foreign Missions to grant but a minor part of what the work demanded, and he was forced to add to his infinitely more important labors those of begging and working to get money, for building, for the printing of a newspaper in Chinese and English, and for supplies of medicine and books, and other evangelistic necessities.

In eight years spent in the great and most interesting home mission fields of the far South and of the upper Mississippi valley, and in the years since 1865, amidst the toils of an office whose end is to raise up and qualify laborers for all the immense harvests which have been referred to, the experience has been the same. The greater and more important work, the preaching of the gospel, and the increase and training of the men who are needed by hundreds

3

where the Church is supplying tens, is ever and ever dragged to the earth by the simple want of that which Christians in America have in abundance to give, but do not give: money.

It has been such necessities as these which have driven the writer first to study, with prayer, every text from the beginning to the end of the word of God which relates in any way to money; next, to inquire into the lessons of the history of the Church of the Lord Jesus Christ since his ascension, to ascertain what have been its experiences as to money; then to look into questions of political economy, national finance, and commerce, which could throw light upon the subject of money.

By these means he has been led to the overwhelming conviction that God has, in his omniscient wisdom, and forethought, and grace through Christ Jesus, made known to the New Testament Church a sufficient Rule for Giving, and the principles which should regulate it. The preparations for it in the Old Testament, the preaching of John the Baptist, the personal teaching and example of the SON OF GOD, the antecedent and succeeding instructions of the epistles and the book of Revelation, have given to this Rule—wonderfully brief as it is, and simple and easy to be remembered, and adapted to all life's way-faring men, so that though fools they need not err therein —a dignity and power which prove that it is divine.

To explain, to illustrate, to impress, and to put into effectual use, for the good of the Church of the Lord Jesus Christ, and for the conversion of the world to him, GOD'S RULE FOR CHRISTIAN GIVING, is the one object of this volume.

In this earnest, practical, and hopeful era, men have sought out and made useful to them the great principles of many departments of physical science, of political economy, now made broader and nobler as "social science," and of moral science. The present seems to be a time for Christians to advance from the past hortatory way of treating the subject, to consider the great principles of religious and ecclesiastical finance, for which perhaps no more appropriate name can be found than that of the SCIENCE OF CHRISTIAN ECONOMY. Upon it depend many momentous questions related to that rapid and general advancement of the kingdom of our LORD JESUS CHRIST, which should now be the great aim and employment of his Church.

CONTENTS.

PART I.

THE DIVINE GIFT OF MONEY.

CHAPTER I.

5

CHAPTER V.

CHAPTER VI.

CHAPTER VII.

PART II.

THE DIVINE RULE FOR THE CHRISTIAN USE OF MONEY.

CHAPTER I.

CHAPTER II.

CHAPTER III.

CHAPTER IV.

CHAPTER V.

CHAPTER VI.

CHAPTER VII.

CHAPTER XIII.

CHAPTER XIV.

GOD'S RULE

FOR

CHRISTIAN GIVING.

PART I.

THE DIVINE GIFT OF MONEY.

CHAPTER I.

GREATNESS OF THE SUBJECT.

"I will shake all nations,
And the Desire of all nations shall come:
And I will fill this house with glory, saith the LORD of hosts.
The silver is mine, and the gold is mine, saith the LORD of hosts.
The glory of this latter house shall be greater than of the former,
    saith the LORD of hosts.
And in this place I will give peace, saith the LORD of hosts."

"They shall not appear before the LORD empty: every man shall give as he is able, according to the blessing of the LORD thy God which he hath given thee."

"Give alms of such things as ye have; and behold all things are clean unto you."

"Covetousness is idolatry."

"Will a man rob God? Yet ye have robbed me,
But ye say, Wherein have we robbed thee?

11

In tithes and offerings.

Ye are cursed with a curse;

For ye have robbed me; even this whole nation."

" Make to yourselves friends (with) the mammon of unrighteousness, that, when ye fail, they may receive you into everlasting habitations."*

Campbell's Translation.—" With the deceitful mammon procure to
yourselves friends, who, after your discharge, may receive you into
the eternal mansions."

IT may be said with truth that the Christian world has
never at any previous time so earnestly directed its
thoughts to the claims and uses of money as it is doing
now. A great necessity is laid upon it by the condition of
the world and of the Church, which is without a parallel in
the past.

It may be said further, that never before have men been
so desirous as now to learn what GOD teaches and commands in the book of eternal truth, with regard to this
subject.

It requires a study of only a limited number of texts, out
of the multitude in the bible which relate to money, to lead
almost any thinking person to the conclusion that no one of
us comprehends and measures the true nature of money,
and its office and importance in the kingdom of God on
earth. Such an examination convicts the Church in modern
ages of failure to employ it in acts of worship and service
according as God has ordained. It reveals the source of an
immeasurable loss to Christians of spiritual strength, of

* Hag. ii. 7–9.   Deut. xvi. 16, 17.   Luke xi. 41.   Col. iii. 5.
Mal. iii. 8, 9.   Luke xvi. 9.

heavenly joy, of comfort amidst earthly troubles, and of hope in death. It brings to light one of the great causes of the vast and abounding iniquity and crime in the world. It shows why glorious and everlasting rewards are promised for the faithful use of money, and why eternal penalties are attached to its abuse.

The subject is so vast, its relationships so extensive, its applications so important, that we are precluded, for the ends of a Manual such as this, the attempt to present more than a summary of the great principles, and of prominent facts necessary to illustrate them, which are plainly related to the particular Divine ordinance respecting the pecuniary gifts of New Testament believers:—"Upon the first day of the week let every one of you lay by him in store as God hath prospered him."

CHAPTER II.

THE ATTRIBUTES OF GOD MANIFEST IN THE CREATION OF THE PRECIOUS METALS AND THE CONSTITUTION OF MONEY.

IN order that mankind in every continent, whatsoever their employments, might fill them with the spirit of religion, and make them practical for its great designs, God created at the beginning and bestowed upon our race an extraordinary gift, that of the metals.

The metals form a department of the Divine work of creation which has performed a most important office in constituting the globe a nobler home for man. They have furnished it with a most effective means for ministering to the happiness, and promoting the education and improvement, of the human family; or, when abused, one for inflicting upon it the judgments of God. A history of gold, silver or copper, or one of iron, tin or lead, would be immeasurably more valuable and interesting to us than the records of any one nation or race that has ever existed on the earth.

The qualities and uses of the metals are vitally related to the supply of most of the common wants of man, to the progress of civilization,* to the support and ceremonies of

---

* Writers on metallurgy insist much on the point that the proficiency in the working, and the extent of the use, of the metals by a nation is one of the best evidences of its measure of civilization.

14

true or false religion in all lands, and even to the general operations of Nature. We are continually more and more surprised at the extent and variety of their presence and influence in all the realms of inanimate or animate matter. They exist in the waters of the oceans which surround the globe; they originate and control some of the most subtle and mighty forces of Nature. They are detected in the analysis of the light which comes to us from the planets, and from stars which are inconceivably remote.

The empire of each metal is distinct, and its Divine ends different. The ancients imagined that they were severally related to the sun, moon, or one of the planets; and that each affected in its own way the health and prosperity of the human race. Gold was the metal related to the sun, silver to the moon, quicksilver to Mercury, tin to Jupiter, iron to Mars, copper to Venus, and lead to Saturn. So powerful and so extensive was this superstition that the astronomical signs for the planets are still used in various countries of Europe by chemists as signs for the metals, and there are multitudes who yet believe themselves and others to be affected for good or evil by those related influences, and consult astrologers with regard to them. Each metal was also associated with a day of the week; gold with Sunday.

Gold is styled "the royal metal." God makes a special claim to it and to silver. "The gold and the silver are mine, saith the Lord of hosts." These two are endowed with the most honorable attributes. They are specially designated as appropriate for offerings to God, and to human beings in the highest authority. They are the most beautiful, brilliant and permanent in color; they are the most easily shaped by

the hammer, graver or mould; they receive the most deli-
cate impressions; and they resist more successfully than
any other metals the destructive effects of time and the
elements.

The properties of these two metals peculiarly suit them to
the purposes of adornment. They are the appropriate setting
of the most costly gems. They are the materials for crowns,
and sceptres, and signets, and all the insignia and ornaments
of priestly and royal office. They are designed to give, and
preserve imperishably, the external splendor and glory of
temples and palaces. They are the substances in nature
which mankind spontaneously shape into forms to express
honor and affection, and to convey pleasure.

But the most important general use for which God gave to
mankind the precious metals was that they might constitute a universal medium of commercial exchange and
standard of material values, and thus be an equivalent and
representative of all the varied and countless products of
human labor. This creates them a capable agency of the
general purposes of human wisdom, skill, enterprise or
power; a means of satisfying most of the wants and desires
of the heart of man as to this world; and a mighty auxiliary in the extension of God's glorious spiritual kingdom
on earth. No temporal gift of God to man is more valuable, gives more evidence of his omniscient goodness, or
should excite in us more gratitude, than that of money.
Let us turn our eyes for a moment upon some of the grand
illustrations of these assertions.

It requires but a limited knowledge of history, and reflection upon it, to learn that everywhere, and in all ages, no

power of civilized society has been so extensive, so subtle, so various, and so mighty, as that of money.

No problems of science have enlisted the interest of the learned and the powerful of all nations and all ages like the two imaginary ones of an elixir of life, and a philosopher's stone capable of transmuting all the baser metals into gold. Researches to discover them may be traced in the history of the most barbarous and most distant races. They are carried on even in the laboratories of this age and of our own country. For to possess the secrets of a source of inexhaustible life and vigor, and of commanding the universal power of gold, would clothe a man with the very attributes of divinity. Had an Alexander or a Napoleon held them, he would inevitably have made the entire globe obey his will.

The governments of the world hold it to be an attribute of sovereignty to coin money. They adjudge it one of the greatest of crimes, and by some of them punishable with death, to counterfeit what is so vital to their existence.

Heathen nations conceive that certain deities inhabit, vivify, and control the tendencies and courses of money. They sometimes coin money in temples, with religious ceremonies. No gods are so generally courted, or feared, as the gods of money, in view of their presumed influence over the welfare and comfort of individuals and families.

Money does indeed seem almost to possess the attributes of divinity. The whole human race bows down to it. There is no one nation or people, the world around, amidst whom pieces of gold or silver coin do not exercise a mysterious charm over men and command their respect and aid in behalf of the possessor.

2

In all the theology of nature we nowhere see more plainly exhibited the glorious attributes of an infinite and beneficent Creator and Governor than in the qualities and uses of gold and silver. The same God made them to subserve the wants of human society who made the blood in the animal organization—that mysterious fluid which penetrates and energizes every separate atom of the body, and both conveys to each its appropriate nourishment and from each its useless secretions or its waste; the same also who in the structure of the world created water, the circulation of which is the life of its vast frame. We see similar wisdom in the wondrous adaptation of gold and of silver—metals which so much resemble each other in their most important requisites, but each of which has yet its own features of excellence—to the grand design of being universal mediums of exchange, and representatives of values. We find in these metals largeness of value in a very small bulk; and the united qualities of malleability, ductility and divisibility, in greater perfection than in any other forms of matter. They easily receive and permanently retain the stamp which certifies to their genuineness, authority and proportionate value when made into coin.

There are no other materials in nature capable of accomplishing the same incalculably important ends. Cattle and sheep, precious stones, shells, iron, the skins of various animals, and other articles, have been set up in different ages and nations as standards of value and common mediums of exchange; but nothing in the various kingdoms of nature is gifted with all the qualities necessary for these imperial ends except gold and silver. The commerce and trade of all countries measure the values, and transact the interchange, of most of their countless materials, according to their equivalents in these metals.

Let us go a step higher. How shall we attempt to estimate or describe the next to omnipotent power which gold and silver exercise in imparting energy, healthfulness, regularity and beneficial results to every form of human industry? Without money, as the means of estimating and exchanging the results of human labor, the forms of labor would be limited and the sum of it would be diminished beyond our power to conceive; a multitude of beneficial manufactures would be extinguished; society would relapse to comparative barbarism. The possession of money develops the manifold resources of nature; it fills a country with every kind of material good; it assists a nation onward in the path of intellectual progress; and it bestows the means of increasing and spreading the benefits and comforts of religion.

The vital power of gold does not perish from age to age. Man, and most of his works, and the fruits of the earth, soon perish; but the piece of money, taken from the hand of an Egyptian mummy, or from the tomb of a king of ancient Babylon, will procure for one rice to-day from the fellahs on the Nile, or myrrh or dates from the naked ryots in India; or it will print the translations of the Scriptures and help to build churches and schools in China or Kurdistan.

Money stoops to sustain and comfort the lowliest. Coins of smaller values than can be conveniently represented by gold and silver are made out of compounds of them with inferior metals, such as copper, zinc, tin and nickel, which possess something of the color and properties of the nobler metals. Thus the poor are supplied with means of carrying on their employments and supplying their wants; and the smaller transactions of society in general are more readily performed.

Even the written decrees of this sovereign are obeyed, and his promises honored, in the most distant countries. His power is an hundred fold magnified and extended by the numerous devices of paper bills, bonds and notes, made payable in the centres of commerce, or bearing interest through the course of many years to come. By such devices does money vastly enlarge its dominion over the whole world.

A reflecting mind is filled with awe, almost with dread, when it considers all these mighty attributes of money. It is next to omnipresent and omnipotent; it exalts and abases nations and men; it seems superior to our short-lived kind. We comprehend the meaning of our Lord Jesus Christ when he ranked it as a god; one who sets up opposition to the true God, reigns supreme over most of our race, and destroys them soul and body for ever. For such is the declaration: "Ye cannot serve God and Mammon."

We see also what Jesus means when he admonishes his disciples to turn what is a tremendous and eternal curse to the unrighteous into a heavenly and everlasting benefit to themselves. "Make to yourselves friends (by means) of the mammon of unrighteousness, that when ye fail they may receive you unto everlasting habitations." * We may, is his meaning, compel the god of this world to make for us

* Matt. vi. 24. Luke xvi. 1–15.

friends and gather for us blessings, which shall mount with us, and fill our heavenly home with companionships and joys which otherwise we should never have known. The men, and women and children, whom our gifts of money were the means of bringing to the habitations above, will make the associations there for ever more blest and delightful.

CHAPTER III.

REWARDS AND PENALTIES CONNECTED WITH MONEY.

IN the earliest appointments for his worship by man the Lord set a great and peculiar sacredness upon blood. It was made a fundamental principle of all sacrifices of animals that "it is the blood that maketh an atonement for the soul." "Almost all things are by the law purged with blood; and without shedding of blood is no remission." The reason is given: "For the life of the flesh is in the blood." *

There is a corresponding sacredness set upon gold and silver money. It was constituted in some sense "an atonement," or equivalent, for human or brute life. "The first-born of thy sons thou shalt redeem;" "because all the first-born are mine." A fixed sum of money was appointed for the redemption of a first-born son, or a daughter devoted by a special vow, or the firstling of an unclean animal, or some other devoted things; the firstling of a clean sacrificial beast could not be redeemed, "it shall surely be put to death." The people when numbered were commanded to give every man a half shekel, the rich no more, the poor no less, as "a ransom for his soul unto the Lord," "that there be no plague among them." This money, the Lord said to them by Moses, is to make an atonement for your souls." †

* Lev. xvii. 11.   Heb. ix. 22.
† Ex. xxxiv. 20.   Num. iii. 13.   Ex. xxx. 15.

22

It is one of the radical principles of political economy that capital and labor are essentially the same. Capital in whatsoever amount represents an equivalent sum of human toil and suffering, which somewhere, and in some way, has been expended in its production. And thus, it may be said, money is blood; money is life. So, as we have seen from the law of the Old Testament, God reckons it.

We are now led, if we have thoroughly weighed the purpose of God in the creation of the precious metals and in the constitution of money, which were presented in the last chapter, another step forward, and have fully brought to view the momentous responsibility to which God holds every man for the use of the money, or property which represents money, in his possession.

Not alone earthly and material blessings and woes, but salvation and damnation, eternal reward and eternal punishment, are suspended upon the condition of the right use or the abuse of money. It is a question of life or death. " Ye are cursed with a curse; for ye have robbed me, even this whole nation." " Bring ye all the tithes into the storehouse, that there may be meat in mine house, and prove me now herewith, saith the LORD of hosts, if I will not open you the windows of heaven, and pour you out a blessing, that there shall not be room enough to receive it." Covetousness withholds oblations from God's altars and treasury; honor and joy from God's service; food and raiment from God's ministers and servants, and from the poor, the widows, the fatherless and the stranger; instruction from the souls of men; and light and life from a world that lieth in darkness and spiritual death. It makes God's mercy, Christ's atonement, and the Spirit's agency, to be of no effect.   Hence God curses it with a great and special curse.   " No covetous man, who is an idolater, hath any inheritance in the kingdom of Christ and of God." *

We are responsible for our brother's life: "Surely your blood of your lives will I require; at the hand of every man's brother will I require the life of man."   We may murder that brother by violence, as did Cain; but we may also murder him by refusing to warn, or to send others to warn him, of danger.   God says, "When I say unto the wicked: Thou shalt surely die; and thou givest him not warning, nor speakest to warn the wicked from his wicked way, to save his life; the same wicked man shall die in his iniquity, but his blood will I require at thine hand." †   The blood of lost men is certainly upon the money of him who does not use it as a steward of God; employing it, next to the necessary maintenance of himself and family, and the discipline and equipments which are required for increase of usefulness, in ways which tend to the salvation of the souls of men.

There are curious white vases of porcelain to be seen in Oriental collections of antiquities, the numerous little cracks in the enamel of which appear to be of a purplish hue.   The explanation which is given for this peculiarity is, that the blood of human sacrifices was cast with them into the kiln in which this costly ware was burned.   Just so the sun lights the lines and crevices of fine mansions, and costly pictures and statuary, and rich tableware and furniture, and even those of unneeded luxuries of the homes of people in

* Mal. iii. 9, 10.   Eph. v. 5.   † Gen. ix. 5.   Ezek. iii. 18.

moderate circumstances, with a purple tinge, the tinge of blood—the blood of misappropriated life, of labor and skill and strength devoted to ends of earth and sense; yea, and the blood of souls unwarned and perishing in Christian and in heathen lands, souls to whom no one has gone with the infinitely precious message: The soul that sinneth it shall die; but the blood of Jesus Christ cleanseth us from all sin.

The penalty of misused pecuniary power is wonderfully like the penalty of misused powers of bodily life. The disordered digestion, the capricious appetite, the enervation and indolence, the tendency to congestion in particular organs, the perhaps sudden and unexpected arrest in death,— these are the symptoms of the enervated and invalid body. They have their precise counterparts in the religious experience of the individual who gives neither means nor toil for the salvation of others, or the building of Christ's Church on earth. They illustrate the condition of congregations and churches which wilt, and fade, and die, under an inward curse of God; just because they sit in spiritual gluttony and drunkenness, luxuriating in pleasant sermons, and prayer-meetings, and revivals among their own children and families, but forgetful of the vast harvest outside, white and perishing, which God has ripened for the sickle, in this and other lands. The "wages" of such sin of omission "is death."

CHAPTER IV.

THE EDUCATION OF MAN AS A SON OF GOD.

THE tender, sleepless, self-denying, patient care of a young boy by an Oriental nurse is one of the most beautiful and touching sights of the Old World. He never appears to weary, all the day and all the night. He carries his little charge lovingly upon his shoulder or back, or in his arms. He shelters him from the beams of the sun, or from the showers of rain, with his varnished umbrella, or great fan. He vigilantly protects him from every possible danger. He liberally supplies him with good food, and pleasant fruits, and refreshing drinks. He recites to him stories; and he teaches and encourages him to be kind and polite, and to behave himself in a proper manner.

Moses takes up this beautiful and impressive illustration, when he addresses his dying instructions to the tribes of Israel. He says: "The beloved of the Lord shall dwell in safety by Him; and the Lord shall cover him all the day long; and he shall dwell between His shoulders." *

There is exhibited an amazing assiduity of tenderness, wisdom and power in God's care of mankind, from the beginning of the world. God seems to have incessantly aimed at the progressive education of man as an immortal

* Deut. xxxiii. 12.

being, and as one destined to hold a place of peculiar honor amidst the vast range and numerous orders of his spiritual creatures.

Paul declares this divine purpose in his Epistle to the Ephesians: "God, for his great love wherewith he loved us, hath made us sit together in heavenly places in Christ, that in the ages to come he might show the exceeding riches of his grace in his kindness to us through Christ Jesus." *

The Son of God gathers us to his heart as "brethren," when he teaches us how to pray. We are to say: "Our Father which art in heaven, thy kingdom come; thy will be done in earth as it is in heaven." The purpose is to teach us that we are to address and love and obey God as one who is truly "our father;" that we are to live on earth as those whose permanent home is "in heaven;" and that we are to employ ourselves and all this life's resources in directing erring and sinning fellow-men to heaven, and in helping to make this earth as like as possible to heaven.

DESIGN IN THE CREATION OF THE WORLD.

We see God's paternal and loving purpose manifested everywhere in the creation of the material world. His great love wherewith he loved us led him to construct a place suitable for the abode of a race which he purposed to make of one family with his dear Son. "He appointed the foundations of the earth,"† "He set a compass upon the face of the deep." "He established the clouds above." He "rejoiced in the habitable part of his earth;" and his

* Eph. ii. 4–7.　　　　† Prov. viii. 27–32.

"delights were with the children of man." The more wide and deep our acquaintance with the whole range of nature, the more amazing appears to us the wealth of those designs which filled the earth with materials formed and deposited to suit the wants of man. Beneath its surface are stored metals, fuel, minerals, of countless kinds and uses; upon it are provided grains, woods, nutritious vegetables, herds of animals capable of domestication ready to serve him, and multitudes of others inhabiting the air and earth and waters, suited to furnish him with all that his appetites or tastes can possibly require. It is warmed and tempered with the glorious sun and air; ventilated and made healthful and pleasant by currents of winds, and rivers and seas; watered with rains, dews, fountains and streams. It is adorned with myriads of varieties of flowers, robed in splendor beyond that of Solomon; and it is made luxurious with delicious fruits. There is no sickness or pain to which man is liable for which some remedy is not devised. On every hand there appear royal preparations for a royal race.

PURPOSES OF THE LEVITICAL DISPENSATION.

The peculiar, intimate and loving tutelage of that family and nation, which when others forsook God continued to serve him, during the ancient patriarchal and Levitical dispensations, affords to us many illustrations of his ultimate gracious purpose in behalf of our race. That affectionate care was ever twofold: it supplied abundantly all the wants of his people and guarded them from evil; and it assiduously instructed them in the way to be holy and useful.

How impressive and valuable is that twofold history—ou the one hand, God leading the nation perpetually, just as he did from Egypt to Canaan, preserving it from all its terrible enemies and supplying its wants by a continued miracle; on the other hand, teaching it by numerous precepts, by impressive appointments of worship and duty, and by many awful judgments, to use rightly, and not to abuse, his temporal and spiritual blessings.

Most impressive among such lessons were many of those which related to the use and abuse of gold and silver. Thus, when God set them free from Egypt, "He brought them forth with silver and gold;" but when they set it up to worship it, he moved Moses to burn it in the fire, and grind it to powder, and strew it upon the water, and make the children of Israel in bitterness and shame to drink of it; he commanded the Levites to go in and out from gate to gate throughout the camp, and slay their guilty brethren and companions and neighbors; thus three thousand were put to death; and lastly, he sent a plague upon the people. When they entered the land of promise and conquered the cities of the heathen, they were specially required to burn their images, and to count their gold and silver a devoted thing which they must not take for themselves, but give to the Lord.   When Achan broke this command, and took a garment and two hundred shekels of silver and a wedge of gold, Joshua and the congregation took these things, and him and his sons and daughters, and his cattle and tent, and all that he had; and they stoned them with stones and burned them with fire.*

* Ps. cv. 37.   Ex. xxxii. 19–29.   Judg. vii.

The stated appointments of the law, as has already been shown, attached to gold and silver a special sacredness to God. The history of the kingdom of Judah and Israel, until their downfall, was ever filled with lessons which were designed to teach them their distinguished position as the chosen people of the Lord of heaven and earth, and to discipline them, as the channel of blessings for the good of the whole race, to holiness and zeal in the use and enjoyment of his munificent temporal gifts to them.

GOD'S WONDROUS PURPOSE OF GRACE IN CHRIST.

But the greatest of all the manifestations of God's "great love wherewith he loved us," and means for the education of man for the grand ends of his creation, is given in the mission of the Lord Jesus Christ. When our race was hopelessly fallen and lost, when all our own efforts for recovery were evidently vain, "God so loved the world, that he gave his only begotten Son, that whosoever believeth in him should not perish, but have everlasting life." Our very ruin was made an occasion for the performance of the most astonishing of all God's acts of condescension and favor to man. At the beginning, the Creator and Lord of the universe had made man a little lower than the angels, he had given him dominion over his works on earth, and put all things under his feet. But now we see Jesus, the person of the Godhead by whom the worlds were made, and who upholds them by the word of his power, come to suffer death for us, and to make reconciliation for our sins, to call and to exalt us to be in an extraordinary sense "brethren;" and we see him rise and sit down on the right hand of the majesty on high, to exercise for us the obligations of that endearing relationship, and to crown us with eternal glory and honor.*

All is done that the Almighty God himself, with his infinite resources, can do to prove to us the validity of our sonship, and the truth of his solemn declaration that literally "ALL THINGS ARE YOURS." We "reign as kings." † He has made us joint occupants of the throne of Jesus. He has made us "sit together in heavenly places in Christ" and with Christ. His purpose is to show to angels and the universe "the exceeding riches of his grace, in his kindness to us through Christ Jesus."

God is solicitous that we should realize and prove this wondrous grace and munificence. He represents its exercise in our behalf to be for his own divine glory. When Jesus Christ was on earth he labored to inspire his disciples with the sense of it, and to instruct them in the duties which it imposed upon them. He said: "Ask and ye shall receive." "If ye shall ask anything in my name I will do it." "Whatsoever ye shall ask in my name that will I do, that the Father may be glorified in the Son." "Take no thought saying, What shall we eat? or, what shall we drink? or, wherewithal shall we be clothed? For after all these things do the Gentiles seek. For your heavenly Father knoweth ye have need of all these things. But seek ye first the kingdom of God, and all these things shall be added unto you." "Give, and it shall be given unto you." "Freely ye have received, freely give." ‡

* John iii. 16.   Heb. i., ii.   † 1 Cor. ii. 21 ; iv. 8.
‡ Matt. vi., x.   John xiv. 13, 14.

As a conspicuous part of the education of those who were at once brethren and disciples, Jesus addressed himself to exhibit in its true light the sin which is in some respects the sum of all sins—covetousness. For as money is the great representative and instrumentality of power in human society, the means of gratifying almost every earthly desire of man, the adored god of the unregenerated heart, so he makes it one of the primary ends of his visit to earth to destroy its magical spell, to lift the souls of believers to a superiority to it, and to teach them in triumphing over the love of it to subordinate it to the beneficent and healthful purposes for which God created it.

Warnings of the Forerunner.

When the forerunner of Jesus was sent to announce that the commencement of "the kingdom of heaven" was at hand, the Jews, in great numbers, from every part of the land, went out to the wilderness to see him. The great theme of his preaching was, "Repent," and "bring forth fruits worthy of repentance." The several classes of men asked, "What shall we do then?" His explanation of what "the fruits" of repentance meant was, in each case, an exhortation to practical charity, and warning against some besetting form of covetousness. The publicans were cautioned against illegal exactions of money. The soldiers were warned against the frauds and violence by which they were accustomed to wring out money from the helpless people. And the people generally were commanded, if they owned but two coats, yet to give up one to the wretch poorer than themselves, and, however small their stock of food, yet to divide it with the hungry. Covetousness was held up as the deadly rot which was at the core of the Jewish religion, and prevented it bringing forth "fruits;" and which would make a holy God lay an axe unto the root of it, and hew down the unrepenting nation, and cast it into the fire.*

Personal Teaching and Monitions of the Son of God.

The Son of God himself, the glorious object of so many centuries of prophecy, at length comes! What are his first acts towards the setting up of "the kingdom of heaven," and the destruction of the kingdom of Satan? He announces his heavenly anointing, as the Messiah, to be especially in order that he may preach the gospel to the poor. The sermon on the mount is opened with a blessing to the poor, and to the poor in spirit; its first woe is to the satisfied rich. He declares the two great antagonistic powers, of good and of evil, to be God and mammon. He declares the first duty of man to be to seek the kingdom of God and his righteousness, and that all needed earthly things shall be added thereto. He declares anxiety for earthly goods to be in its nature heathenism: "For after all these things do the gentiles seek." He enters upon his first observance of the passover, after he begins his ministry, by scourging the money-changers out of the temple. He teaches his disciples to pray; and the first three requests offered are for the prevalence of the spiritual kingdom of God upon the earth, and but one out of the seven petitions has reference to bodily wants; and those are then considered only with reference to the passing day, and as to

* Luke iii.

the simplest necessaries of life.   He sends the apostles, and
the seventy disciples, to preach the gospel, heal the sick,
cleanse the lepers, raise the dead; but his most emphatic
charge is, not to carry gold, or silver, or even brass money,
nor any superfluous raiment.   A rich young man seeks to
learn of him the way to obtain eternal life: he tells him,
first " sell whatsoever thou hast, and give to the poor."
He feeds thousands in the wilderness, and satisfies them
from a handful of barley biscuit, to show his power to provide all necessary good.   His most angry warnings are
uttered to the men who built great storehouses and barns,
and cared not for their souls.   His most striking parables,
such as those from the pearl-merchant, the treasure-hunter,
and the dishonest steward—his most touching lessons from
nature, the lilies, the birds, the foxes—his most surprising
miracles, the draughts of fishes, the finding of money in the
fish's mouth, and the instantaneous relief of the poor, the
blind, the leper, for the mere asking,—all were one incessant
testimony against covetousness as to worldly possessions, and
in favor of submission, obedience and trust in God.   " He
that forsaketh not all that he hath cannot be my disciple."
His most eminent model of Christian beneficence is a poor
widow, who casts into the Lord's treasury her last and only
farthing, "even all her living."   His life was at once life-
long beneficence and poverty.   He reserved on this world
which he made, but which knew him not, nowhere a safe
refuge, like the foxes; no quiet nest or home, like the birds.
He washed, like the humblest of the household slaves, the
feet of his own followers.   And when he describes, with
Divine foreknowledge of all its particulars, the coming great

Day of Judgment, he says, that the chief ground of accusation and damnation of worldlings and false professors will be that they withheld time, strength and property, from those acts of mercy to the hungry, the thirsty, the stranger, the sick, the prisoner, of which he was the great example, and the performance of which is the principal evidence and seal of the divinity of his religion; while the acquittal and salvation of the righteous will be chiefly on the ground of such evidence as the performance of those acts affords of their sincere belief in and obedience to him.*

To any one who, with an open and sincere mind, will consider the life and teachings of the Lord Jesus Christ, they will appear a grand heavenly lesson of beneficent charity; and a continued and burning protest against the love of earthly possessions, springing from the love of self, as the great enemy of love to God, and as the great obstacle to the salvation of the race of man through his own death. What an example, when the highest of all became the lowest of all, and he who alone was rich for our sakes became poor; when, indeed, he gave himself, and the King of kings took upon him the form of a servant for us, and suffered for us the shameful and agonizing death of the cross! †

INFLUENCE OF THE HOLY SPIRIT ON THE CONDUCT OF BELIEVERS.

We may complete this sketch of the divine education of man in sonship toward his Divine "father," and in the use of his gifts as becomes a spiritual and immortal being, if we

---

* Matt. v.–vii. Mark x. 21. Luke xiv. 33; xxi. 1–4; ix. 58.
John xiii. Matt. xxv.   † 2 Cor. viii. 9. Phil. ii. 5–8.

consider the effects of the operation of the Holy Spirit upon the conduct of believers.

When the Spirit of God opens the eyes, turns darkness into light, breaks the chains of Satan and brings men to God; when he convinces and assures them of the riches and glory of their inheritance, and of their power to command "all things" through the intercession of Christ; and when he fills them with godly indignation, fear, vehement desire and revenge—with the intense emotions of the soldier who hates the kingdom and power of Satan, and is ready to sacrifice everything he possesses in order to destroy them and to place his adored sovereign, the rightful Lord of all, upon his earthly throne—how wholly, how extremely different from what they were in a state of unbelief are their conceptions and feelings in regard to the nature, uses and ends of money! Those men were not drunk with wine, but "filled"—yes, thirsty souls to whom God gave of the heavenly fountain of the water of life so that they were *filled*—"with the Spirit;" who at Pentecost hastened to sell their possessions, and distribute to the bodily need, while they ministered to the boundless and perishing spiritual need around them. Angels indeed such men and women were! And with such heavenly pictures of the perfected results of God's purpose in the instruction and discipline of man, the inspired history of the Church is finished; and it is placed in our hands, to study and to imitate its examples until the end of time.*

And here again God sets the precious jewel of grace, so pure, luminous and adapted to the crown of the King, in

* Eph. i.   2 Cor. vii. 11.   Acts ii.

a black foil.   We behold the swift and dreadful curse which falls upon Ananias and Sapphira who "keep back part of the price" of what they had vowed to God, and "lie not unto men but unto God."   Thus righteousness and truth are seen ever to meet and walk with mercy and peace.   Thus the first manifestation of the glorious power and joyfulness of the gifts of the Holy Spirit is accompanied by the most terrible warning of the penalty of abusing and perverting them and God's instrumentalities of good to the world.*

THE GREAT PRINCIPLE AS EXPLAINED IN THE EPISTLES.

The epistles of the New Testament bring clearly to view the great principle upon which God is acting in the education of man.   A household among the great family of his intelligent creatures has fallen into rebellion and utter ruin; the father would restore and reinstate it in the love and honor of "the whole family in heaven and earth."   The greatest sacrifices, the most patient and wise means, must be employed to accomplish this end.   It would be of no use to restore its external privileges without such an education as will elevate its nature, ennoble its affections, and inspire it with the realization of its position, its dignities, its responsibilities, its duties, and its destinies.   Each member must be, in fine, lifted from the place of an animal to one higher than an angel's. He must be fitted to be "*a child of God.*"†

Take in now the full breadth of the plan.   It is not to restore one man, not one nation.   It is to restore *mankind.* It is to bring back the race, and to teach it to have royal dominion over the creatures, and the portion of creation

* Acts v. 1–11. Ps. lxxxv. 10.   † Luke vi. 35. Rom. viii. 17.

which God has assigned to it.   It is to make it lord over all
the realm of matter; and to teach it to use in holiness, wisdom and love, the divine faculties and the material gifts
committed to it.

Nor doth it yet appear what we shall be, when this mystery of godliness, this earthly education of the "brethren"
of the SON OF GOD, has been perfected. Eye hath not seen,
nor ear heard, neither have entered into the heart of man,
the things which God hath prepared for this princely race!
And it is yet among the deep things of God, how he will
surprise by them the lofty principalities and powers in
heavenly places, in that hour when a new glory shall be
added to his name by that which shall be revealed in us; and
when "the creation itself shall be delivered from the bondage
of corruption into the glorious liberty of the children of
God!"*

Human language can say no more than this. Human
thought cannot rise higher than this. Here we must stop,
and each of us wait, it may be groan, earnestly desiring to
be clothed upon with better faculties, when mortality shall
be swallowed up of life.   "*Then* shall we know!" †

* 2 Cor. ii. 7–12.   Eph. iii. 8–10.   Rom. viii. 18–22.   † 1 Cor.
xiii. 12.

CHAPTER V.

DEVELOPMENT OF PECUNIARY BENEFICENCE IN THE CHRISTIAN CHURCH.

IF we would thoroughly comprehend and feel the greatness of the subject of Christian giving, it is necessary that we should take at least a brief glance at the history of the Church since Christ, and the developments of God's providence as there exhibited.

The history of the Christian Church has been marked by five distinct stages in the growth of the principle of beneficence. Each one of these stages, like those in the development of a fruit-bearing tree from its first germ in the earth, has accomplished some purpose of God's providential wisdom.

These progressive stages may be dated from the eras of its implantation by Christ and the apostles; the emperor Constantine; Hildebrand, pope Gregory VII.; the great Reformation; and the final expansion of Christianity, upon which we are now entering. Each one of these stages is necessary to the production of the great results which God has in view.

In the first stage we see its miraculous, swift and vigorous dissemination. In the second, the effort of the kingdoms of the world, convinced of its divine potency, to seduce it into an alliance with themselves, and employ it to subserve

their aims. In the third, the converse ambitious effort of
the Church to humble and rule the world, by the means of
its acquired power and wealth. In the fourth stage, the
view presents us with a mutual revulsion, the Church cling-
ing by faith, wrecked, naked and wounded, to the rock
Christ Jesus, fearing and scarce able to attempt the building
of the temple which God has decreed shall surmount that
rock ; while the world defiantly mocks her, and treats her
celestial mission, and demands and expectations, with scorn.
The final stage in the Church's history exalts her to the
position in which God's gracious purposes in her are fulfilled ; she sits as a queen, rich in the affections and obedience of a sanctified world.

FIRST STAGE.— CHRIST AND THE APOSTLES.

The first stage of Christianity was one of wondrous energy,
and of extraordinary interest to all succeeding ages and to
all races and generations of men. Then the vitalizing power
of the ministry of the Lord Jesus, succeeded by the influences
of the Holy Ghost, operates like the warm sun and quickening rains of the spring season upon the implanted seed. It is
saturated with heavenly influences. It swells and is leavened
with a new power. The Church is filled with a faith which
moves it to undertake the speedy conquest of the whole
world to Jesus Christ, its Redeemer and Lord.

It was the confident expectation of the primitive Christians that the entire world would in a short time be converted.
Such seemed to be the promise of the Old Testament.
David, whose royal son the Lord Jesus was commonly styled
,by the Jews, had said, "He shall have dominion from sea to

sea, and from the river unto the ends of the earth." Isaiah, who had with most wonderful clearness described his ministry and suffering for sin, had in triumphant and rapturous language described the fruits of them. His advent was compared to the rising of the sun upon a world wrapped in deep thick darkness, so gloriously that all nations and kings should come and gather themselves together to enjoy the blessings of its light. When all the objects of Christ's mission to earth were accomplished and he was ready to return to heaven, he gave his disciples their final instruction and commission: "All power is given unto me in heaven and in earth. Go ye therefore, and teach all nations; baptizing them in the name of the Father, and of the Son, and of the Holy Ghost: teaching them to observe all things whatsoever I have commanded you: and lo I am with you alway, unto the end of the world." The divine dignity and authority of Christ were attested by his transfiguration. The ability to fulfill these vast promises, and give superhuman success to the efforts of his disciples in obedience to his commands, was corroborated by his miracles. The outpouring of the Holy Spirit with such overwhelming power that thousands of people were converted under a single sermon, was intended to illustrate that infinite ability, and the willingness to exercise it.*

The zeal thus incited led the primitive Christians to exercise a charity and liberality which has been the astonishment and admiration of the world until this day. Even their enemies acknowledged how great it was, and how power-

* Ps. lxxii. 8.   Isa. lx.   Luke ii. 32.   Matt. xxviii. 18–20.   Mark xvi. 20.   Acts ii.–v.

fully it affected the souls of all men. The emperor Julian the Apostate exhorted the pagans to establish houses for the relief of the sick, strangers, and the poor; saying to them, "It is a shame for us that the impious Galileans should not only keep their own poor but even many of ours, whom we leave to suffer." They gave, in weekly contributions, sums of money proportioned to their ability, the aggregate of which was immense. This was spent in the performance of acts of charity, which relieved the sick, taught the youth, fed the hungry, redeemed captives and slaves in all lands, supported the ordinances of religion, and sent the gospel over the entire world. The recompense of this heavenly zeal and charity was the conversion of great multitudes from every nation to the Christian religion. "It embraced," says the heathen Pliny, writing to the emperor Trajan, "persons of all ranks and ages, and even of both sexes;" and it was "not confined to the cities only, but spread its infection among the country villages." Irenæus declared that it had "extended throughout the whole world, even to the uttermost bounds of the earth." Eusebius, writing the history of the early Church, affirms that "through a celestial influence and co-operation, the doctrine of the Saviour, like the rays of the sun, quickly irradiated the whole world. In accordance with divine prophecy, within a little time the sound of his inspired evangelists and apostles had gone throughout all the earth, and their words to the ends of the world. Throughout every city and village, like as in a well-filled granary, churches soon abounded, and were filled with members from every race of people."*

* EUSEB. PAMPH.; *Ec. Hist.;* II., iii.

The abuse of this all-abounding faith and virtue, or energy, was as the apostle Peter foresaw and admonished them, that they did not add "to virtue, knowledge; and to knowledge, temperance," that is, discipline and firmness.* The defects of the primitive charity of the Church of Christ were the want of comprehensiveness, of system, of judgment and of large intelligence. Blazing and glorious as was this first kindling of the Christian flame, the time had not come for the construction of the enginery for which such zeal would again, at a future day, be needed, in order to the accomplishment of God's grand final designs, in the casting down of every high thing and every stronghold of Satan's powerful kingdom on earth.

The lessons which this first stage of Christian beneficence suggests are, the greatness of the gifts of the Holy Spirit which are yet in store for the fullness of times in this dispensation; the efficacy of prayer; and the power and energy of individual believers when clothed with the Holy Ghost; and it presents us with the highest illustrations of complete and true consecration to the ends of Christ's atonement, embracing life, offspring, property, all that a man hath, losing life here that he may gain life for ever.

SECOND STAGE.—ERA OF CONSTANTINE.

The second great era of the Church, that of Constantine the Great, brings to our view one of the most remarkable figures in the world's history; that of a Roman emperor, apparently converted from heathenism to Christ, seeking to govern the spirits of men by civil law, and to renovate society and convert the world by the political authority and

* 2 Pet. i. 5.

resources of the empire. Constantine divided the Church
into great primacies and episcopates of provinces and of
cities, just as he divided for political purposes the territory
of the empire, assigning to each its suitable officer. He exempted bishops from subordination to civil jurisdiction and
yet gave them power to exercise authority as judges in civil
cases, and required the civil officers to carry out their decis-
ions and mandates. He destroyed, or altered, the idol
temples; commanded Sunday and Friday to be publicly
observed as religious days; and carried in his military
campaigns a tent designed for religious worship. He con-
vened, and sometimes presided over, councils of the bishops
and clergy; and prohibited by law heretical opinions, and
the exercise of the worship of God by heretics. He wrote
to the Council of Tyre urging upon its members "that sin-
cerity and fidelity which, according to our Saviour, ought to
pervade all our actions. Nothing shall be omitted," he
says, "on my part to further the interests of our religion." *
He applied the ordinary revenues of the empire to the designs of the Church; ordered churches, asylums for widows
and orphans, and hospitals for the sick, everywhere to be
built and maintained; and directed copies of the Scriptures
to be transcribed and distributed. He liberally supported
the clergy, and levied taxes and tribute that were to be put
into their hands for religious and charitable uses. He coined
a great quantity of idols of silver and gold into money; and
purified others by passing them through the fire, and presented them to the churches. He transferred the seat of
the imperial government from Rome to Constantinople, in

* THEODORET; *Ec. Hist.* I. xxix.

order thus to assume a new and more favorable position, that he might command greater power over the three continents, and rear a new Christian metropolis of the world. "And," says an ancient church historian, "his wishes were not thwarted; for by the assistance of God it became the most populous and wealthy of cities. I know of no cause to account for this extraordinary aggrandizement, unless it be the piety of the builder and of the inhabitants, and their compassion and liberality toward the poor."* He made from the nails of the cross of Christ, which his mother Helena sent to him from the sepulchre at Jerusalem, a headband and bit for his horse, which he inscribed, according to the prophecy of Zechariah, with the words: "HOLINESS TO THE LORD."

Was this second grand experience of the Church, its adoption by the State, and support by the State, to capacitate it for its sublime mission on earth? No! The Church was convulsed internally with Arianism, which rejected the very divinity of Christ; and was torn with numerous other controversies. The character of its great patron, Constantine, was doubtful and inconsistent. Some of his letters to councils and the clergy express admirable Christian sentiments. But his faith was mixed with superstition and his acts with the idolatry of favorite gods. He slew his son Crispus, perhaps his wife Fausta, and several others of his own kindred. He resisted Christian baptism, for questionable or superstitious reasons, till near death, and the ceremony was then performed by an Arian; and it is still uncertain whether he was not always at heart a pagan, or an Arian. His son

* SOZOMEN; *Ec. Hist.* II., iii.

Constantius was an Arian and opposer of the truth. His nephew, the infamous Julian the Apostate, who was the following emperor, endeavored to exterminate Christianity, and to rebuild Jerusalem in order to give the lie to the last prophecies of Jesus Christ himself. The character of Constantine to be intelligently apprehended must be compared with that of the emperor Charlemagne of France, or that of Peter the Great of Russia ; men of giant energy, passions and will, full of contradictions, but raised up at great junctures of human affairs, for the accomplishment of extraordinary designs of divine Providence.*

The effects of Constantine's efforts to subordinate the Church to the advantage of the State, and of his extravagant appropriations from the civil revenues to her support, were pernicious to religion. The clergy were inflamed with the love of property. In succeeding centuries, they amassed by solicitation from the temporal powers, through separate taxation, and by means of a multitude of devices, an incalculably vast amount of every sort of landed and material possessions. They employed fraud and forgery when necessary to their ends. A most famous forgery was that known as the Donation of Constantine, to Pope Sylvester and his successors,

* GIBBON's estimate of Constantine is, as usual, gross and onesided. NIEBUHR is severe upon him. He says (*Lectures on Roman Hist.*, III., 303) that "his religion was a rare jumble," and that "to call him even a saint is a profanation of the word." STANLEY is more discriminating; he closes a just and eloquent portraiture of Constantine's life and character (*History of the Eastern Church*, Lect. VI.) by holding it up as a compound of "Pagan and Christian, orthodox and heretical, liberal and fanatical, not to be imitated or admired, but much to be remembered, and deeply to be studied."

of "the sovereignty of Rome; of the provinces, cities and towns of the whole of Italy; and of the Western regions."

Many of the wisest and purest members of the Roman Church in every age have deplored the secularization of Christianity by Constantine. What he designed to be a mutual advantage to the Empire and the Church became the degradation and destruction of spiritual religion.*

Those truly spiritual men who from century to century lifted up their voices in cries for reform, down to Huss and Wickliffe, attributed to Constantine the transformation of the Church from its primitive simplicity and purity. The "Old Catholics," the latest schism from the Papacy, say concerning its temporalities, that in addition to the evils of the "well-meant, but ill-advised munificence of Constantine," the forgery of his so-called Donation, was a "large and inexhaustible treasury from which political and municipal privileges could be drawn just as they were wanted."†

The Waldensian and other anti-papal churches, or indi-

* Thus, according to JOHN MILTON, *Reformation in England*, b. I., the poet DANTE exclaims :

"Ah, Constantine! To how much ill was cause,
Not thy conversion, but those rich domains
Which the first wealthy pope received of thee."
Inferno ; xix. 115–117.

And ARIOSTO compares the grandeur of the Church to
"a flowery mountain green,
Which once smelt sweet, now stinks as odiously.
This was the gift, if you the truth will have,
That Constantine to good Sylvester gave."
Orlando Furioso ; xxxiv. 80.

† DOLLINGER ; *Fables respecting the Pope in the Middle Ages.*

viduals, were driven to the opposite extreme of sentiment with regard to ecclesiastical possessions; they argued that all investments and funded property are essentially corrupting, that religion must be maintained entirely by free will offerings, and that it is the scriptural duty of the clergy to continue poor. The English Puritans held up the provision of Constantine for the Church in her days of feeble youth as that of "a nursing father who overlaid or choked it in the nursing." *

The experiences of the British Protestant churches are singularly valuable and instructive to us in respect to their efforts to ally themselves with the State in such a way as to derive from it the benefits of secular law and maintenance, while they yielded in return those of religious services and instruction to its subjects. In the Episcopal Established Church the political sovereign is its legal head, and the government appoints its officials. In other bodies various degrees of subserviency have existed. The seceders from the Scotch Established Church, who formed in 1842 the Free Church, had desperately but all in vain struggled to unite dependence on the State with fealty to the interests of Christianity; or, as the Rev. Dr. Chalmers said,† to "harmonize the principle of a national establishment of Christianity with the principle of spiritual independence." The long and painful series of disruptions and disestablishments, is leading the British people, and should assist us in America, to discern that the divine plan for the maintenance and

---

* MILTON, *The Likeliest Means to Remove Hirelings out of the Church;* Prose Works, II., 146.

† HANNA; *Life and Writings of Chalmers,* IV., chaps. vii., etc.

spread of religion is not State grants and patronage; nor yet is it that unregulated "Voluntaryism" to which the leaders of the Free Church disruption earnestly objected as insufficient and unreliable. It is the perfect plan which is revealed, though long overlooked, in the New Testament.

THIRD STAGE, ERA OF HILDEBRAND.

The third great stage of Christianity, that beginning with the papacy of Hildebrand, pope Gregory VII., reveals to us the Church stronger than the State—the pope claiming that all kings and kingdoms, their religious and their civil law, and all their property and interests, were subject to him; distributing thrones and possessions as the earthly vicegerent of God.

Amidst the frightful disorders, irreligion and dissoluteness of the Middle Ages, we can clearly trace the origin of the doctrines and practices which created or allowed them to one grand source—that "root of all evil" of which Paul spoke to the early Church. The imperious "lords over God's heritage," in that period of terrible darkness and iniquity, "fed the flock of God" "for filthy lucre."* The doctrines and offices of religion were all erected into a grand engine for getting money. The distinctions of classes and grades of venial sins, as distinguished from those sins which are mortal, were parts of it. Hence the imputed value of works of merit; the commercial estimates as to penances for sins already committed, and those as to indulgences even for sins which men purpose hereafter to commit.† Hence the as-

* 1 Tim. vi. 10. 1 Pet. v. 2, 3.

† A volume was published in London, in 1674, entitled *"Taxes*

sumed efficacy of certain forms of worship and of prayers in a dead and unknown language; and the superior sanctity of a priesthood, its isolation from society, and monastic and ascetic practices. Hence the doctrines of purgatory and limbo; and the consequent pecuniary value of extreme unction for the dying and of masses for the dead, and of prayers to canonized saints and to angels.

"All things," said the old proverb, "can be bought and sold at Rome." The churches of the city of Rome—so huge, so gorgeous, so rich, so beautiful, so adorned with all that earthly wealth can procure, that the most splendid palaces of emperors and kings look mean and worthless compared with them—what an exhibition they are of the proceeds of that dreadful merchandise of all things costly and delicious; and that merchandise of slaves, and souls of men; the merchandise of human virtue, of the truth of

of the Apostolical Chancery," etc., which contains many tables of the cost of bulls, dispensations, pardons, etc. *Anthony Egane* gave a list of many pages of the regular prices, which were fixed at Rome before the Reformation for the benefit of the people of Ireland, of dispensations for all imaginable kinds of sin. Thus, "If either father or mother, sister or brother, do strangle or smother an infant, they are to pay £4, 2s." To kill a bishop, cost £36, 9s.; a priest, £6, 2s.; a father, mother, brother or sister, £4, 1s., 8d. The dispensation of an oath or contract, £7, 2s., 3d. See *Quart. Rev. of Amer. Prot. Ass.;* July, 1845. The same privileges were granted to other nations. At the valuation of Tetzel, in Germany, "polygamy cost six ducats; sacrilege and perjury, nine ducats; murder, eight; witchcraft, two." At that of Samson, in Switzerland, "infanticide" was rated at "four livres tournois; parricide, or fratricide, at one ducat." *D'Aubigné, History of Reformation,* Book III.

God, and of the blood of prophets and saints; which in one hour shall be brought to desolation! Well may the apostle cry: "Rejoice over her, thou heaven, and ye holy apostles and prophets, for God hath avenged you on her." *

There is no sight on all the face of the earth so dreadful as those wonderfully magnificent churches and religious edifices of Rome. . The Saviour of men pronounced his most terrible woes upon the "hypocrisy and iniquity" which built the tombs of the prophets and garnished the sepulchres of the righteous, but was within full of extortion and excess; upon the men who themselves "are like unto whited sepulchres, which appear indeed beautiful outward, but are within full of dead men's bones and all uncleanness." † Then how immeasurably great and dreadful must be his condemnation of the hypocrisy and iniquity which have reared those vast monuments of long ages of fraud, practiced not on one small nation but on the whole race of man, of avarice insatiable, of crimes untold, of the waters of the cup of salvation converted into deadly poison, of the gospel of the grace of God to all lost and ruined souls turned into pictures, statues, mosaics, gems, and every form of enchanting luxury and delight of the eye, the ear, and every carnal sense.

This third great era conveys, in God's providence, a lesson which the people of God can never, must never, forget. It is the frightful picture of the dominion of *mammon* in the house of God! It is the lesson of the culmination of the lust for superiority of place, for refinements of knowledge and speech, for luxurious edifices of worship and

---

* Rev. xix.   † Matt. xxiii. 27-29.

charity, for stained windows and ornamented walls, and for exquisite music. Rome for centuries has had them all, so grandly that any competition of ours is vain apish mimicry. But what has she with them? "How much she hath glorified herself and lived deliciously, so much torment and sorrow give her. Therefore shall her plagues come in one day, death, and mourning, and famine; and she shall be utterly burned with fire: for strong is the Lord God who judgeth her." *

To every Protestant people, to every sincere spiritual soul, how plain, how sufficient, should be the practical conclusion from this great divine lesson.

* Rev. xviii. 7, 8.

CHAPTER VI.

ERA OF THE REFORMATION: ITS BENEFITS.

WHAT was the immediate divine purpose toward the Church in the fourth era of its history, that of the Protestant Reformation? Preparation, discipline, organization.

The lesson of the first era, we saw, was the power of the Holy Ghost. That of the second era, the evils of an alliance between the two, in which the State is superior to the Church. That of the third era, those of an alliance of the opposite kind, in which the Church is superior to the State. These are the three great experiences which are necessary to prepare the Church for the fourth era, which commenced with Luther, and is yet in progress. The lesson of it is the duties, the power, and the final honors, of her single and sincere allegiance to JESUS CHRIST as her almighty Head and King. She learns to discipline and organize all the boundless resources which she finds that he bestows upon his faithful followers, with the supreme determination to make him the LORD OF ALL.

The illustrations of the preparation of society and the Church for the coming reign of Christ are so numerous, and every one in its place so interesting, that the briefest consideration of them would swell this volume far beyond its

proposed limits. We can only suggest the leading topics
which may be studied, thought upon, and their relations
to personal duty and to the obligations of the Church
prayerfully considered.

The *first* manifest result of the Protestant Reformation has
been a restoration of spirituality of faith. This is illustrated
by the history during the past four centuries of such subjects as the following :

The successive translations of the word of God into the
common languages of nearly all nations.

The restoration of purity of doctrine. The definition,
and systematization, of creeds. The exploration of Oriental literature. The elucidation of Scripture by acquaintance with the geography, productions, etc., of Palestine
and neighboring lands.

Re-establishment of spirituality of worship. Abandon-
ment of symbolism; of unnecessary ecclesiastical forms; of
liturgical worship.

Reassertion of the right of private judgment. Personal
and domestic use of the Scriptures. Associations of the
laity for prayer and the advancement of religion. Cultivation of personal responsibility to God.

The large gifts of the Holy Spirit in extensive revivals of
religion.

The progressive quickening of the Churches of Christ
with the spirit of missions; with desires for the salvation,
and spiritual improvement, of men of all classes and conditions.

The *second* class of benefits resulting from the Reformation is that related to the intellectual improvement of mankind.   We group under it such topics as these:

Universal awakening of the human intellect preparatory, and subsequent to, Reformation.

Revival of learning.   Boundless enlargement till now.

Prevalence of sounder principles of reasoning.   Rise of inductive method in philosophy.   Immense and ever-increasing influence upon all departments of science, and the employments of men.

Invention of printing; variety of applications; inestimable advantages.

Progressive extension of education to the common people.

Development of national systems of taxation for education and for objects connected with intellectual improvement of society.

Improvement of educational literature.   Introduction of rational methods of instruction.

Elevation of practical departments of knowledge in education.   Illustration of themes of instruction by material objects, by applications of various arts, by painting, photography, the camera, etc.   The popular lecture system.   Immense influence of hymns and music adapted to children.   Science of school architecture.

The rise, world-wide diffusion, and power, of Sabbath-schools.

The relief of the several afflicted classes of society; its literature, methods, benefits to the objects, and humanizing effects upon society.

Forms of popularization of literature; cheap multiplication of them by the press.

The *third* powerful effect of the Reformation was the awakening of men to their political and social rights. Hence we are led to inquire into the following subjects:

The gradual development of true principles as to the inherent rights of man. Overthrow of theory of the divine right of kings, and of various false political systems and oppressive usages.

Establishment of constitutional and representative forms of government among the various nations of the world.

Concession of right of suffrage to all classes of society; its effects upon the degraded and ignorant.

Reforms in legislation. Reforms in penal discipline. Diminution of capital punishments.

Improvements in police systems.

Abolition of slavery in different countries; by peaceful emancipation, as in British, Portuguese and Spanish colonies, Russia, Dutch possessions, Siam; by war, as in the United States, and the effects of that war upon other nations, even the most remote.

We look under the *fourth* head for matters connected with the improvement of the physical condition of the human race.

This naturally leads us to observe the grand results which have flowed from the geographical discoveries of this era; the discovery of America, and vast benefaction of arable and mineral territory to the human race; discovery of the passage to the East by the Cape of Good Hope; revolutions caused by shortening of commercial communication with ancient nations of the East.

Effects of cutting and bridging by railroads the great isthmuses of Suez and Panama.

Discoveries of coal; domestic use; uses for manufactures. New and innumerable applications of iron * to beneficial ends; those of other metals.

Invention of steam and other motive powers as to their manifold practical applications in facilitating labor and multiplying its proceeds.†

* A bright young Chinese, who had been well educated at one of our mission schools in his own country, on his return from a visit which he made to America, was asked what had most struck him in the appearance of our cities? He answered, one thing was the great abundance and variety of the uses of iron. It must ever astonish a person from Oriental lands, where their usages are still those of the early or Middle Ages, and where they rarely use even common nails of iron, to see this most difficult of the common metals to work applied to architecture, ship-building, railroads, bridges, massive machinery, telegraphy, and almost every conceivable want of ordinary life. It should be remembered by us that almost all this has come with the present century.

† It has been estimated that the steam power of Great Britain alone equals the combined manual labor of one third of the population of the world. The proceeds of the industry of the entire race are fully doubled by the machinery which the capital of the several nations of Christian Europe and America has placed in the hands of its people. Within those great centres of manufacturing activity men now virtually live three times as long, perform three times as much labor, and enjoy more than three times as much of the benefits of human toil and skill, as did their fathers of a century ago. Many particular individuals and communities have risen to a relative position, as compared with those of times past, which can hardly be estimated.

Means of illumination of dwellings, streets, and places of public convocation ; gas; petroleum; chemical possibilities of far more powerful agencies.

Improvements in clothing. Machinery for weaving various materials. Increase of cotton. Invention of sewing machine; rapid spread over the world; effects on uncivilized nations.*

Variety, exchange and increase of agricultural and horticultural productions. Fertilizers. Machinery for reaping, mowing, etc.

Instrumentalities for the relief of suffering. Inestimable improvements in medicine and surgery.

Discoveries of prophylactics; vaccination; quinine.

Systems for alleviation of natural calamities. Life insurance. Savings banks. Fire insurance. Fire engines and associations. Marine insurance.

Sanitary improvements. Water supply of cities. Sewage of cities.

Interment of dead in rural cemeteries.

A *final* class of means in the Divine hand for preparing mankind for the coming kingdom of Christ includes the agencies for the universal diffusion of the benefits which are conferred. Under this may be grouped the following:

Invention of railroads; wonderful extension over all

---

* The writer was greatly impressed in visiting some of the islands in the Pacific Ocean, and the Indian Archipelago, to observe how Christian missions and Christian commerce put our clothing upon uncivilized races. Thus we comprehend the final mission of the sewing machine.

countries. Application of steam in locomotive. Improvements in comfort and safety of traveling; sleeping cars.

Use of steam in propulsion of vessels on water. Improvements in sailing vessels.

Universal interchange of useful products; commercial facilities; commercial associations and agencies.

Introduction of newspapers. Benefits of the religious press. Inventions for illustrating papers and books. Uses of lithography, photography, etc., in the dissemination of knowledge. Advantages to heathen races.

Facilities for postal communication. Cheap postage. Transportation of books, seeds, etc., by mail; extension to most distant nations.

The electric telegraph; various methods in telegraphing; trans-oceanic communications; extension around the whole world.

Centralization of commerce in hands of Protestant Christian nations. Moral and religious causes of decline of commerce of Venice; Portugal; Spain; Holland. Causes of unparalleled increase of commerce of Great Britain; of Germany; of the United States of America.

Just as the great fact of the approach of the morning sun accounts for ten thousand others in every department of nature, in air and earth and sea, in the vegetable and animal and even mineral kingdoms, in the movements and employments of mankind, in things that affect the welfare of every man, woman and child; so that greater fact that "the kingdom of heaven is at hand" accounted for the innumerable ways in which the Old Dispensation was prepared for the manifestation of the Son of God to suffer for sin, and accounts for those greater and more impressive ways in which this New Dispensation is prepared for the reign of his glory.

PECULIAR FINANCIAL BENEFITS OF THIS ERA.

In pondering and trying to estimate the relations of money to the stupendous movements of this era, we are deeply impressed with several great benefits to mankind which attend it.

The first financial benefit of this era has been the immense and increasing influx of the precious metals from its commencement until the present time. During the first half of the century following the discovery of America there was an average *annual supply* of about three millions of dollars; during the last half it swelled to eleven millions. The following entire century averaged sixteen millions. The first half of the last century brought in over twenty-two millions a year; the last half over thirty-three millions. The first quarter of the present century averaged more than fifty-four millions. But vast and rapid as was the increase in three centuries, that is, from an influx of three to one of fifty-four millions a year, it suddenly doubled that rate at the middle of the present century. Since then a deluge of the precious metals has been poured into the New World, and into all the Old World by the vast discoveries of them in California and the states and territories east and south of it, in Mexico and British America, in Australia and New Zealand, in the Ural Mountains of Russia, in Eastern Siberia and in other parts of the world.

The *total amount* of the precious metals in the world is

estimated by some of the best judges* to have been previous
to the discovery of America two thousand millions of dollars; at present, about ten thousand millions, which is
nearly equally divided between gold and silver. About
three thousand millions of this is in coin.

This continually swelling flood has unsettled, and as a
whole lifted to a higher level, the whole structure of modern
society, and powerfully affected all the ordinary employments and interests of men, even in the most distant and
isolated countries. They have been heaved and moved by
a strange power which they did not comprehend. They
have been waked to influences which before had no control
over them. The whole world and all its institutions, has
been shaken and changed by the rising of this deluge of gold
and silver. As to material agencies, an eminent authority
upon these subjects says:† "there is but one way of really
improving the condition of the laboring class, and that is by
increasing the ratio of capital to population." This is not
a sound statement; but measured by this standard, the facts
we have mentioned with regard to the influx of the metals
which are the basis of capital are an important indication of
rapidly maturing and most beneficent purposes of God with
regard to the general condition of mankind.

Another great financial benefit of the present era is the
different forms and extensive use of the credit system. The
vast multiplication of money by the modern banking system,
the development of the resources of countries by associated

* HUMBOLDT, McCULLOCH, JACOBS (*Hist. of Precious Metals*), and
information from the United States Mint, Philadelphia.

† McCulloch.

capital issuing its bonds and inviting investments bearing a regulated interest, the manifold applications of insurance, the hypothetical transfer of capital for commercial payments of any amount, even in distant countries, by paper draughts, or by telegraphic orders, the stability and power imparted to governments by the power to issue bonds payable in future time—these and many other applications of the modern credit system form an element which is of incalculable importance to the industry and commerce of the world,* and to the supremacy of Christian civilization among its nations. It is a means of the greatest importance to the supply, and to the safe transfer, of the pecuniary means which are necessary to the evangelization of remote nations.

It is a third distinguishing characteristic of the influx of wealth in this era that its beneficial effects have been most abundantly felt by the poorer classes of society. The propheeies of the reign of the Messiah which promise its blessings most abundantly to the poor, and to "the children of the needy," are truly beginning to be fulfilled. Their condition has been elevated far more than that of others in the general rise. The several great classes of spiritual, intellectual, political, social, and physical benefits, which we have·considered as resulting from the Reformation, have been distributed in the valleys and plains of society, and have only partially reached the higher grounds. Thus said Isaiah: " the city shall be low in a low place."†

* " Excepting the merest retail business, not one per cent. of the payments of Great Britain and the United States are made in real money." COLWELL, *Ways and Means of Payment;* p. 2.

† Ps. lxxii. 4. Isa. xxxii. 19.

CHAPTER VII.

DEFECTS OF THE REFORMATION, AND THEIR RESULTS.

WHEN scrutinized merely as a religious movement there appear two great defects in the Reformation itself. Unless we consider these we can hardly understand the pecuniary failures of Protestantism, and their remedy.

THE GREAT DOCTRINAL DEFECT.

The Reformation was a mighty revival of religion; the first of the great "latter-day" outpourings of the Holy Ghost which are to convert the whole world; the angel "flying in the midst of heaven, having the everlasting gospel to preach unto them that dwell on the earth, and to every nation, and kindred, and tongue, and people." * The first Pentecost regenerated a great number from the ancient Jewish Church, which was then finally abandoned to formalism and destruction; this second one redeemed millions from the Christian Church when the same spiritual death, like that of winter to the landscape, had fallen upon it. In the experience of the believers of the second Pentecost there is much to remind us of that of the converts of the first.

The first great outpourings of the Holy Ghost filled the souls of Christians with intense emotional enjoyments, which

---

* Rev. xiv. 6.

led some to neglect the practical duties of their profession. The public performance of these duties, indeed, marked men and women as victims for heathen persecution. For these and other reasons it became necessary for the apostle James, "the Lord's brother," to address to the churches a general epistle teaching the necessity of good works as the fruit and evidence of true faith. The epistles of Peter also are to be understood much in the same light.

It is a fact of great significance, in studying the lessons of Church history, that the intensity of Martin Luther's apprehension of the doctrine of justification by faith alone, and the energy of his opposition to the all-prevalent formalism about him, so unsettled his judgment and his ordinary docility of obedience to Scripture, that he fell into the gross error of denying the authenticity and authority of this epistle of James. He says: "The epistle of James I do not consider as the writing of an apostle at all. . . . It ascribes justification to works, in direct contradistinction to Paul and all the other sacred writers. . . . James enjoins only the law and works; and so confuses the one with the other that it appears to me as if some good pious man had caught a few sayings from the disciples of the apostles, and committed them to paper. Or it is possibly written by another person from his preaching."

The Scriptures principally teach not only "what man is to believe concerning God," but also "what duty God requires of man." The latter co-equal and vital part of the word of God was imagined to be inconsistent with the doctrines of grace. Andrew Carlstadt held the view of the Lord's Supper, since retained by the Socinians, that it is only a commemorative ordinance. Neither Luther nor Melancthon sufficiently valued the authority of the Sabbath itself, as binding in this dispensation. There are many such evidences that the general tendency of the Reformation at first was to depreciate the obligation of the positive ordinances of Christianity.

There was then in the sentiments of the men of that great period a grand defect which has been felt throughout the entire body of the Protestant Churches, which continually refresh their faith and zeal at these sources. The result as to the duties connected with the theme of beneficence which we are now considering would plainly be that, however definitely and positively stated, an ordinance relating to the contribution of money, the source so largely of the dreadful abuses which the Reformers were laboring through Christ to remove, would probably be regarded with disfavor, or entirely passed by as not obligatory.

THE GREAT PRACTICAL DEFECT.

A second grand defect in the power of the Reformation was of a practical character. It arose from an extraordinary peculiarity of this great revival, namely, that there was no immediate need, comparable with its extent and effects at least, for money to build churches, and establish schools and colleges, on account of the immense confiscations of monkish and episcopal property, which had been accumulating for centuries previous in the hands of the Roman Church. Hence an appointment of the New Testament respecting collections of money would not press itself upon the consideration of the Protestants; and provisions for

5

them worthy of the obligations and ultimate aims and glorious hopes of the kingdom of Christ would not be made.

THE REFORMATION GAVE ENERGY TO ROMANISM.

One effect of the Reformation was a very memorable one. While the good men who had rescued the truth, amidst the homes of their fathers, from the dungeons and chains of ages, were content to improve there their victory, Romanism yielded that field only to set herself to far wider and easier conquests. The establishment of the order of the Jesuits, the reinspiration of the Dominicans and Franciscans with a zeal for foreign missions, and the subsequent rise and activity in missionary fields of the Lazarists and some other orders, saved her from ruin and made her really stronger than she was before.

The influence of those two grand original defects as to the money power, a means absolutely essential to growth and extension, has been vitally and disastrously injurious to all subsequent Protestant Christianity. Romanism has continuously despatched its bands of missionaries over the world; but Protestant churches, previous to the present century, aimlessly sent forth here and there an individual. Romanism enlisted men of learning and experience, and even of rank; she munificently equipped them with astronomical and other scientific apparatus, that is of inestimable value in overturning the superstitious notions of the heathen and disposing them to listen to the truths and overtures of the gospel. The foreign missionaries of Protestant churches have been volunteer striplings, fresh from the theological schools, unproven, and scantily furnished with needful instrumentalities.   Romanism, as the consequence, even after the catastrophes of the Reformation, has again thoroughly aroused the affections and disciplined the strength of her people ; while Protestantism, until reanimated by the revivals and missionary zeal of the present century, has exhibited unending disruptions and disintegration.   Romanism till of late seemed entirely to have arrested at least the geographical extension of Protestantism.   The general impression which the consideration of Protestantism leaves upon a reflecting mind is, that only the merciful power of God preserves it ; that by Romanism is, that had it only *that* power, its compactness, its discipline, its confidence, and its effectual control of the pecuniary means of even its humblest members, would send forth its legions triumphant over all the earth.

We are able to trace in history, very clearly, the twofold results—those affecting the Church within and without—which flow from the neglect to use for the glory of God and for the good of mankind the benefits which God has so abundantly granted to her.

MISIMPROVEMENT OF GOD'S BLESSINGS THE BLIGHT OF THE CHURCH WITHIN.

Looking *within*, we see that God has turned the blessings which he has bestowed into a curse to the churches themselves.   He has greatly multiplied their wealth.   Just as the vital force of the heart impels the circulation of the blood in the whole body, so the great Governor of the world has ordered it that the Protestant Christianity of the world controls at this time its riches.   The gold and silver, the exchange, the scientific and inventive skill, the manufactures, the commerce, the military and naval power, all the accompaniments of national wealth, receive the pulsations which cause them to circulate from pole to pole, here in the Christian centre. These are temporal blessings which result from the comparatively higher morality, justice, intelligence and industry of races which are enlightened by Divine revelation.

But as riches have increased they have "set their heart" upon them. They have loved them, and honored them, and coveted them, and made them their god. They have forgotten the words of Christ: "No man can serve two masters: for either he will hate the one and love the other; or else he will hold to the one and despise the other. Ye cannot serve GOD and MAMMON." Jehovah, who gave as the first commandment, "Thou shalt have no other gods before me," gave as the last, "Thou shalt not covet." For this great and capital sin God cursed the ancient Israel. He says, "For the iniquity of his covetousness was I wroth and smote him; I hid me, and was wroth; and he went on frowardly in the way of his heart." This sin is made the evil and abominable thing, which God hates, of the New Testament dispensation; for "covetousness is idolatry." And "no covetous man, who is an idolater, hath any inheritance in the kingdom of Christ and of God." *

The reason of God's great anger with covetousness is that it is finally but the *love of self*. It is the desire for the most effective means to accomplish the will and purposes of self; the rebellion of self against the sovereign claims of God. This deadly corruption of our nature comes forth in a great

* Isa. lvii. 17.   Col. iii. 5.   Eph. v. 5.

many different modes of manifestation. Just as the cancerous disease in the bodily system takes forms so numerous and so unlike to each other, the scarlet fungus, the cheesy tubercle, the foul ulcer, the purple stain, the white scirrhus, the wart on the skin, the nodule on the bone; so with the multiform shapes in which this general poison of the spirit may exhibit itself. A man may say "I am rich, and increased with goods, and have need of nothing; and know not that he is wretched, and miserable, and poor, and blind, and naked."* Independence as to God's providence, blindness as to God's judgments, haughty contempt of God's service, rejection of the truth of God's word, neglect of prayer, are but different symptoms of the conceit of superiority to human necessities which the possession of, or even passion for, money produces. In man's relations to man it comes forth in pride, the indulgence of lusts, injustice, oppression; the determination, without regard to consequences, to get money, is the origin of falsehood, cruelty, theft, murder.

"Wide wasting pest! that rages unconfined,
And crowds with crime the records of mankind."†

In the low, dark, unhappy condition of the souls of the larger part of the professed Christians of this age; in the unprofitableness of the labors of most ministers compared with what the infinite power of the gospel in their hands, and the glorious promises and primitive examples of its success, would lead men to expect; in the incessant taunts of

* Rev. iii. 17.
† Dr. Sam. Johnson; *The Vanity of Human Wishes.*

enemies and the triumphant assumptions of infidels; in the
dissensions of believers and churches—in all, we trace at
bottom chiefly the results of the love of self, and the want
of a true and entire consecration of Christians, in soul, and
life, and possessions, to the glorious ends of the kingdom of
Christ Jesus their Lord.

CALAMITOUS INFLUENCE OF PROTESTANTISM WITHOUT THE GOSPEL UPON THE NATIONS OF THE WORLD.

Let us turn and take a view of Protestant Christianity
from *without*. If any one will take the trouble to acquaint
himself with the opinions of thinking men of other creeds
and nations, he will often be surprised and healthfully
humbled to find how different is their estimate of the good
which Protestantism has accomplished from that which we
commonly entertain.

The condition of the classes that dig the coal and iron and
tin of England, that spin her cottons, that reap her harvests, was, until within one generation, too bestialized and
wretched to contemplate without horror. The few pro-
prietors and nobility were enormously enriched, while the
poor from whose toils their wealth came were not better
cared for than the brutes; were prevented by the system of
law from obtaining the control of any part of the soil;
lived a dependent, ignorant, animal existence; and an
almost incredible share of them finished their days as miserable paupers in the public poor-houses. The English
theories of political economy have largely given shape to our
own. The continental writers of Europe have cried out
with horror against the primary definition of it, as the

science of the production and distribution of wealth, and the declaration that "wealth, not happiness" is its chief concern; as if provisions for morals, human wants and comforts, individual sufferings, and the education and improvement of the masses, were not fundamental duties of the society upon which Providence bestows wealth.*

When one compares the amount of money which the immeasurably less wealthy populations of European and Asiatic countries give for religious objects with that from the vast prosperity and abundance which reigns in America he must be distressed. Protestant consciences seem to have divorced commercial, manufacturing and agricultural enterprises from the duty of practical returns to God—in gifts proportionate to their remunerativeness, for the advancement of his kingdom on earth—or to man, in donations and labors to communicate the knowledge and blessings of the gospel. The nations with which we traffic abroad commonly speak of us as irreligious materialists. Our commerce, our railroads, our factories, our sciences and arts, our ordinary business employments, seem almost to exclude from them the idea that men owe all their wealth and prosperity, all their material, national and social blessings, to God; and that they are under obligation to render to the Lord, for *all* his benefits, a just and becoming tribute.

One of the most painful and deep impressions made upon the mind of a Christian who visits Eastern nations, and learns their sentiments and usages, is that of the compara-

* The theories of Smith, Malthus, Ricardo, and other English writers have been earnestly reprobated in this country by Henry C. Carey, Stephen Colwell, and Frederic List.

tive *godlessness* of Protestant commerce with them. The ancient commerce of India with Burmah, Cambodia, the Indian Archipelago, Tibet, and China, made them Buddhists; and they remain so till this day. Go where he will around the world, even in San Francisco or New York, the Buddhist is not ashamed of his religion. The Buddhist merchant visits the temples of the gods upon whose particular aid he depends, and makes offerings and burns his written prayers to them, when he engages in an important commercial enterprise; if it be successful, he pays an oblation of money to the priests, with which they may print religious tracts, or repair an altar, or purchase provisions; or he may possibly, if rich, erect a building for a school, or pave a road, or construct a bridge. Mohammedan merchants are till this day zealously carrying the Koran with their caravans into the idolatrous countries of Asia and Africa. Within recent years, they have peacefully converted to their faith nations of Central Africa, which have only known of England and America by the manufactured cottons, the weapons of destruction and the intoxicating liquors, which they have received chiefly in exchange for slaves, and to enable them to make war for the capture of slaves. The swarthy Parsee fire-worshipper might have been seen, generation after generation, going out in his white robes at sunrise or sunset, from his counting-room in the seaports of China and other countries foreign to him as to us, in order to worship the Deity as represented by the sun. The traveler might have had there the opportunity to observe that one of those enterprising merchants, instead of taking out a policy of insurance, as he is solicited by our people to do when he sends forth a vessel, or consignment of goods, prays instead to the divine source of life and good for his favor and blessing, and piously goes out into the public streets and squares of the city and distributes a quantity of copper money, in charity, to the poor, the blind and lepers. Through all the Middle Ages Romanism sent forth in the footsteps of its merchants devoted men and women to convert heathen nations.* Wherever its commerce has gone since the Reformation, it has planted large and well-appointed missions. They exist in every continent. Vessels like the "Stella del Mar"— the Star of the Sea—long preceded the English ship Duff, or American "Morning Star," as missionary ships amidst the islands of the Pacific. But it is astonishing and dreadful to see how godless, how licentious, how covetous, how

---

* The pious spirit of much of that mediæval commerce is beautifully illustrated in the narratives of those memorable voyages which brought to light this new hemisphere. Every one who has read them remembers how, in setting sail, Columbus and his officers solemnly invoked the protection of God; how he commenced his journal of the first voyage "in the name of our Lord Jesus Christ," and at his first step upon the newly discovered land, "threw himself on his knees, kissed the earth, and returned thanks to God with tears of joy." He called the island by the name of the Saviour (San Salvador). On his return, the court of Spain joined in offering up a devout and grateful tribute of praise, "giving glory to God for the discovery of another world." Columbus, in the confident expectation of great riches, "made a vow to furnish within seven years an army, consisting of four thousand horse and fifty thousand men, for the rescue of the holy sepulchre at Jerusalem, and a similar force within the five following years." IRVING; *Life of Columbus*, books IV. and V.

unmerciful, Protestant commerce has almost universally been.

It is one of the terrible facts of history that Britain and America maintained commercial intercourse with some of the principal heathen empires of the world for two or three hundreds of years, but made scarcely an effort to instruct those from whom we were drawing vast wealth and earthly benefits, in regard to their duties to their Creator, and the way of pardon for sin and life eternal through Jesus Christ.

ILLUSTRATIONS IN EASTERN ASIA.

That truly great and humane statesman, Edmund Burke, in 1783 described the character of the British East India Company's government in India until his day. He said of its servants: * "They have no more social habits with the people, than if they still resided in England; nor indeed any species of intercourse but that which is necessary to making a sudden fortune, with a view to a remote settlement. Animated with all the avarice of age, and all the impetuosity of youth, they roll in one after another; wave after wave. There is nothing before the eyes of the natives but an endless, hopeless prospect of new flights of birds of prey and passage, with appetites continually renewing for a food that is continually wasting. England has erected no churches, no hospitals, no palaces, no schools; England has built no bridges, made no high roads, cut no navigations, dug out no reservoirs. Every other conqueror of every other description has left some monument, either of state or beneficence, behind him. Were we to be driven out of

* Speech on Mr. Fox's East India Bill.

India this day, nothing would remain to tell that it had been possessed, during the inglorious period of our dominion, by anything better than the orang-outang or the tiger." In opening the impeachment of the Governor General, Warren Hastings, he said: "The whole of the crimes charged upon Mr. Hastings have their root and origin in avarice and rapacity. . . . His very merits are nothing but merits of money; money got by oppression, money got by extortion, money got by violence, from the poor or from the rich.   There is breach of faith, cruelty, perfidy; yet the great ruling principle of the whole is money. His acts are acts, and his government a government, of money. It is base avarice, which never can look, by any prejudice of mankind, anything like virtue. . . . In short, money is the beginning, money is the middle, and money is the end of his government."

In India Britain has been compelled by a just and merciful God, through the rebellions which would otherwise have overturned her valuable empire there, as well as by the spiritually awakened conscience of later days, to establish equitable laws, the beginnings of educational and humane institutions, and Christian missions.   But to this day there continue some of the greatest abuses, by which she annually reaps scores of millions of pounds sterling from the labors and sufferings of the nations which she has compelled to yield to them at the mouth of the cannon. One of these is the opium trade. Opium is raised by the British government in India that it may be exported to China, to pay there for teas and silks, which could otherwise only be obtained for specie. To legalize this diabolical traffic, so ruinous to

China, she made almost continual war upon that empire for a quarter of a century.

To make these general statements creates no distinct impression upon the mind of the reader. They must be studied in their details, and influences, and consequences. For this we have little space here. Yet it is important to our present object to consider for a moment one of the strangest, saddest scenes which our world has ever witnessed. It occurred upon a Chinese war-junk. A "Christian" nation was deluging the coasts of that heathen empire with blood, and blackening them with the burned ruins of its own cities, because the aged and humane emperor would not consent to the introduction of "the opium poison" among his subjects. After a battle near Canton, a party of English sailors, who boarded a war-junk from which all had fled save the wounded and the dead, beheld the commander, a brave and intelligent man, who was much esteemed by his own people, seated lifeless by the cabin table. His fresh blood was streaming over his Buddhist rosary and down his richly embroidered blue satin robe. Before his glazed eyes there was spread out an open Chinese book. The assailants looked with wonder to ascertain what it was. It was a missionary translation of the Gospel of John. The unhappy man had been searching for information as to the secret of the terrible energy and success of the cruel and wicked race with whom he was vainly contending. He had found some of their books which were translated into his own tongue. And there he sat, murdered by them, his perplexed eyes fixed upon the Gospel of John!

How strange and dreadful a spectacle! For many centuries Christian nations had been trading and sending embassies of state to China; but then for the first time it is that millions upon millions begin to find that they possess *any* religion, or belief in a state of rewards and punishments, or sacred books. Since, before our great Reformation, ships had gone there by the Cape of Good Hope; and they had yet only known us in their common language as "devils," "pirates," and "monsters." At that particular time to which I have alluded Christians were smuggling by violence into their country the astounding amount of thirty millions of dollars' worth of opium each year; and spending a few thousands of dollars at Canton, and a few tens of thousands at ports outside of the Chinese dominions, in giving to the Chinese people the gospel. There were three men at Canton and twenty-five elsewhere engaged in teaching them the mercy of God; while a great and powerful fleet of vessels of war and many merchant vessels, were inflicting the cruelty, the lust, and the wrath of man. Some things in the scheme of redemption "the angels desire to look into;" but if there be ever tears in angelic eyes it must be when they look upon such a scene as that of the cabin in which a crowd of men from a Christian nation stood astonished at those outspread hands, cold in death, grasping helplessly the Gospel of John; and at the stony eyeballs, blinded in death by our weapons of destruction while they pondered the mysterious words: "Peace I leave with you, my peace I give unto you. Let not your heart be troubled, neither let it be afraid."*

This was truly a representative scene. The bewildered, slaughtered "heathen," and the powerful invading "Chris-

* John xiv. 27.

tians;" the few pennies to give the gospel, the millions of pounds to carry on war; a few scattered individuals engaged in preaching, teaching the youth, and healing the sick, but grand fleets and armaments and armies to spread rapine and death, to compel the admission of opium, or rum, or corruption in even worse forms, and to make the name of Christ abhorred by the gentiles. This is a picture which is representative of our relations in America to the Indian and the negro; of those of England in her influence in India and China, and Caffraria and Australia; of those of Holland in the great islands of the East Indies. It is continually, over and over again in a thousand fields, the scene of the murdered mandarin with the Gospel of John.

QUESTION OF THE BALANCE OF GOOD OR EVIL.

We close this review of the era of Christianity which commenced with the Reformation of three centuries ago by observing that, great as have been many of its' benefits to the Church of Christ and to mankind, its defects, as represented in the influence of the nations which have accepted it upon the world, have been lamentably great; and the results until the present time have in some respects been so tremendously disastrous, that the external influence of our intercourse with the chief heathen nations of the world has done them fully as much of injury as of good.

We saw the failures of Christianity in its preceding stages. Now, in its turn, Protestantism has not accomplished the grand designs of the gospel of the Lord Jesus Christ. The Eternal Son of God came into the world to make himself an offering for sin, to bear our griefs, to heal all human woes;

yet he cries, speaking prophetically of the Church *until our time:* "I have labored in vain, I have spent my strength for nought and in vain."* When we take a comprehensive survey of the condition of the thirteen hundred millions of mankind in the habitable parts of the globe, and allow the utmost probable estimate of the very small number amidst all its races and nations who possess, and spiritually understand and obey, the word of God, we must confess that now, eighteen centuries after the agony of Gethsemane and the blood of Calvary, Sin still reigns, moral Death reigns, the powers of Hell reign, in all the earth.

And yet Protestantism has *not* been a "failure," as some have boldly declared. It has been a long and cold and stormy spring-time. The green blades have put forth only here and there on the face of the earth, and in sheltered spots. But there is a great harvest near. These three grand centuries have been an era of all-important preparation, discipline, and organization; the ends of which, in their financial aspects at least, the Church is just beginning to conceive.

* Isaiah, chaps. xlix. to liv.

PART II.

THE DIVINE RULE FOR THE CHRISTIAN USE OF MONEY.

CHAPTER I.

THE NECESSITY FOR A DIVINE RULE FOR CHRISTIAN GIVING.

THE solemn question often comes up in the secret thoughts of every genuine Christian, at times appalling and terrifying him with the additional consideration that he must answer it publicly in the Judgment Day: Why is the religion of the Lord Jesus Christ so unsuccessful in converting mankind? His reasoning will follow some such channel as this: " I see not the one-twentieth part of our race accepting that simple gospel which at the beginning seemed about to possess the globe, and but a small portion of these becoming truly spiritual Christians. After coming triumphant out of persecutions, intended to exterminate it in fire and blood, I find it betrays Christ to the world for its lucre; then that it rises superior to the world, not to instruct and purify it, but to enslave it, to plunder it, and to glut itself with sensual gratifications. I see it granted, since the Reformation, a great revival of spirituality of doctrine; and a wondrous wealth of knowledge, and of all that constitutes secular power, poured upon the churches of Western Europe and America: and yet, since this apparent resurrection, three centuries and a half more have passed away without that Christianity having extended its dominion much beyond the races which at that time accepted it. What is the defect, that the mighty gospel does not sweep like a great wind, from pole to pole? It cannot be in the power of God, which is infinite. It cannot be in the willingness of God, who sent his Son to die for sinners, and who is not willing that any should perish, nor, much more, that whole nations should go together to eternal destruction. Then it must be in man. If in us, it must be either in the want of believing prayer, or of consecrated men, or of sufficient pecuniary means. I can scarcely say that the defect is in the amount or themes of prayer, since God has so inspired the language of Scripture that we can hardly use its words and sentiments at all in prayer without asking for the extension of his kingdom, and power, and glory on earth. As to the spirit of prayer, that will be regulated largely by our labors for its ends. So I am bound down to the conclusion, that the great hindrance to the salvation of the world is chiefly in the want of the personal consecration of Christians to that end; that men and women who can give life do not give their life; that men and women who cannot give life, but can give money, do not give money. There must, then, be far more laborers to go forth, and those who stay must feel that their part is to give to them the means to prosecute

6

their heavenly work. Otherwise the talk of converting the world is mere trifling with the souls of men, and a mockery of God."

Shown by the Chief End for which God made the Precious Metals.

It was shown in a former chapter that the precious metals, especially in their adaptation for use as money, are a most important part of the material creation, and among the most honorable and valuable of the Divine gifts to mankind. Let us consider now the chief and most important end for which they are to be used.

"The heaven is my throne, and the earth is my footstool." "For all those things hath mine hand made, saith the Lord." The chief end of all beings and things that he has made is to show forth his glory; to be "for a name, and for a praise, and for a glory." * This is the great end for which he made gold and silver, or what men may agree to accept as pecuniary equivalents redeemable in them. They are appointed first for royal tribute to him. They are the general medium for the exchange of the products of man's labor, to his glory. They are the representatives of the materials necessary for the sustenance of life in his service, and for the maintenance of the war against evil in which Christians are engaged. His Church needs money; for to say this is merely another form of saying that ships, cars on railroads and other vehicles, are necessary to transport the bodies of the soldiers of Christ, food necessary to nourish them, clothing and houses necessary for their physical

* Jer. xiii. 11. Isa. lxvi. 12.

health and comfort, church and school buildings necessary for converts, books necessary to convey truth, medicine necessary to heal the sick, and that the all-wise God has so organized man and society that while the Holy Spirit is the great source of power in all good, man must do his part, must co-operate through earthly materials; and if this be not done, the whole machinery of grace must stand still. Money is the social instrumentality by which all these materials are procured; by which alone the varieties of human labor necessary to furnish them can be put in operation. The very existence here of those wholly engaged in the service of the Church depends upon the possession of the ordinary means of supporting it. They are not superhuman. They are men, with the wants of men. And while they are so, there is no means by which they can obtain the necessaries of life, comfort, or enjoyment, for themselves and their families, without giving a common and acceptable equivalent for the labor which others have spent in producing or providing them; that is, money. If then the God of nature has made the precious metals, which are so important a department of nature, for his glory, their use should be made truly and greatly to glorify him. He should be honored by a system of giving, just as he is by regularity in almost all else that pertains to his worship and service. It cannot be expected that he can be pleased with fitfulness or carelessness, or bless what is given to him in this way any more than he can bless these habits in the farmer who tills the soil, or the laborer in any ordinary calling.

PRESUMPTION THAT THE OMNISCIENT HEAD OF THE
CHURCH WOULD REVEAL A PECUNIARY SYSTEM FOR
ITS MAINTENANCE.

It is in perfect accordance with God's wise and gracious
methods in governing the world for us to expect that he
would reveal in the Scriptures a system for contributions of
money, from all his people, for the grand objects of the
Church of the Lord Jesus Christ.   If God so organized his
Church on earth that the conversion of the world is to be
accomplished, not by visible or audible displays of his divine majesty and power, and justice and mercy ; nor—what,
if it had been left to us to plan, we would have judged
necessary—by the continuous agency of orders of beings far
superior to us in love, knowledge, holiness, and strength ;
but so that man must be the instrument of saving man, and
his ministers and servants be as subject as are their fellow
men to all the necessities of their earthly nature ; then
would he leave this kingdom without some sufficient arrangement as to the means of supplying the wants of those
ministers and servants?   Would he, whose government of
nature here, and its counterpart in the material heavens, is
so wonderfully perfect, not reveal to his Church some
method according to which his subjects should furnish
the means needful to carry on the great warfare of the
kingdom of his Son against sin?   It would surely be an
anomaly in God's government were this not the case.   It is
incredible that a Being who saw the end from the beginning,
and foreknew the world-wide wants of the Church in the
New Dispensation, which displays " to the principalities and

powers in heavenly places the manifold wisdom of God,"
would not make some earthly arrangements to meet those
wants. It would throw discredit on the authority which
calls some of our race to special and official service, and
lays them under the stress of obedience to his commands,
did not God lay upon other members of it the burthen of
some definite ordinance as to the share they should bear in
the common duty. And in the plan of revelation, which
shuts out all such topics of communication from heaven as
are irrelevant to the kingdom of Christ, but which is so
very clear and full in regard to it, it would surely be a
signal and lamentable defect were this vital point of human
agency left without the light which men there so much
need. So that look at what attribute of God we will, or at
the wants and instrumentalities of his kingdom, or at the
designs of his word, we are forced to expect that he would
reveal some general system in regard to the consecration and
employment of our money.

THE SPIRIT OF THE OLD TESTAMENT PROVES THE NEED OF SUCH A SYSTEM.

The spirit of the Old Testament revelations confirms the
presumptions drawn from the attributes, works and manifest
general purposes of God. If any man out of a sincere desire to learn and to do his duty will consider it, he will see
that certain spiritual and everlasting principles underlie what
is ceremonial, typical and temporary, in the law of Moses.
When he dispossesses his mind of all previous misconcep-
tions in regard to the spirit of the Old Testament, and
studies it critically and thoroughly, this we conceive must be

the prevailing impression he receives: that God designed by
it to teach that religion is *a business*, the great business of a
human being; that the ordinary employments of men must
be all made subordinate to their spiritual interests; and that
a liberal share of the pecuniary proceeds of those employments
must be devoted *by a regular method* to the maintenance
of his service.   The particularity of the laws with regard to
tithes, first-fruits, oblations, sacrifices, the exact numbers
and kinds of the various animals to be offered, the precise
quantities of the flour, oil and wine, the necessity and fixed
rates of redemption and forfeit, and the careful designation
of the times for the performance of public religious duties,
all seem designed to teach that, just as in the appointments
which prefigured the ministry and sufferings of the Saviour
for men *he* "fulfilled all righteousness,"* so on the part of
those who *are* saved there must be complete and universal
consecration of themselves and their possessions to God,
and regular and devoted employment of every kind of
agency at their command to the great ends of Christ's mission to a lost world.

THE TEACHING AND GOSPEL OF CHRIST BASED UPON AN IMPLIED SYSTEM.

We turn for further light to the personal instructions of
the Great Teacher, who came down from heaven, and has
made known to us the things which he heard of the Father.†
Three features of Christ's teaching seem to us most prominent: that he makes the power and joy of religion to lie so
greatly in personal love to himself; that so large a share of

* Matt. iii. 15.   † John iii. and xv.

his instructions have reference to *duties*—the sermon on the mount and other formal discourses being chiefly of this character; and that he rates so high the measure of *results* expected of us. His favorite illustration is taken from the productiveness of the fruits of the earth, which in the case of good seed regularly multiply themselves, some an hundred-fold, some sixty-fold, some thirty-fold. There must evidently be inferred from such lessons an immensely greater consecration of the resources of believers, and a corresponding multiplication of the agencies of evangelization, before such measures of increase can be attained. The Lord Jesus saw that the principal stumbling block to the spread of his gospel was covetousness. He warned his disciples to beware of covetousness; classed covetousness, as a sin, with adultery and murder, and exclaimed, "What shall it profit a man if he shall gain the whole world and lose his own soul?" His instructions as to the use of money, so far as the idea of a formal element entered into them, were based upon, and calculated to perpetuate, at least the radical principles of the Old Testament in regard to systematic contributions for religious purposes. The parables of the ten talents, the five talents, the lord of the vineyard to whom the fruits are denied, the unjust steward who deducts from the account of one debtor five-tenths and from that of another two-tenths, of the Pharisee who trusted in the *merit* of his tithes and despised others, and many other such lessons, exhibit this character. And, while Jesus warns his disciples against the danger of self-righteousness in giving money according to a regular system, just as he does in regard to that in connection with prayer, or fasting, there is not a word to intimate that the act itself was otherwise than commendable and a duty, when performed from the right motives. His warnings are all in the opposite direction. He says: "Think not that I am come to destroy the law, or the prophets: I am not come to destroy, but to fulfill." "For I say unto you, That except your righteousness shall *exceed* the righteousness of the Scribes and Pharisees, ye shall in no case enter into the kingdom of heaven."* These words teach that it will be a fearful thing in the judgment for the multitude of nominal Christians who *do* so much less, and *give* so much less, than did the Jews, though they profess to be governed by a higher law.

We are met here with the declaration of Paul: "Ye are not under the law, but under grace."† Now, what does this mean? If a Christian step from a height, *because* he is a Christian will he not break his neck?—if he put his hand in the fire, will it not be burned?—if he sink in the sea, will he not be drowned?—then he is certainly under the laws of nature. If a Christian rob, or commit murder, will he not be punished?—then he is also as certainly under the moral law, both to God and to man. How is he then "not under the law?" He is simply not under it as a principle, or motive, of obedience. That is, he is governed by a *new principle*, which is not fear, but love; not the terrors of Sinai, but the melting power of Calvary. As Paul explains, he is a man who dies as to the old nature, and lives again in a new and higher one; the principle of life, the inward law, is a new one. Or, he is like a woman whose former husband is dead, and she married to another; the

* Matt. v. 15–20.   † Rom. vi. 14.

submission is the same though the law is a different one. In each case the essence of law, service, and also recompense or punishment, inheres.* Now the "love of Christ constrains," impels and controls him; but surely not to less activity and consecration than did the old law. The "Christian" cannot labor less for God, or give less to his cause, than did the Jew.

Every point of comparison between the necessities and aspirations of Christianity and those of Judaism puts to shame the thought that "Christians" can fail here. Christianity has far greater wants than Judaism—the wants of an advanced and more cultivated age of the world; the wants of an incomparably more varied machinery; the wants of a vigorous resistance to far more numerous, active, and skillful enemies; the wants of immensely greater populations, and more debased, in Christian lands; the wants of a whole world which is to be speedily conquered for Immanuel. God has given in the New Testament a spiritual and sufficient ordinance adapted to these great ends. And the low, unsuccessful, humiliated condition of that kingdom on the earth, its woeful failure after eighteen hundred years to conquer more than a few limited districts of "the world," "*all*" of which should, according to the last command of Christ, now be subject to it, lies, so far as human duty is related to it, largely in the mistakes and neglect of the Church as to the obedience which she owes to the fundamental law as to the contributions and co-operation of "every one."

* Rom. vii.

GREAT NECESSITIES OF THE PRESENT ERA, LIKE THOSE
OF THE ERA OF CHRIST, MANIFESTED IN THE DECAY
OF FALSE RELIGIONS.

The present condition of the world is in many remarkable
respects similar to what existed when Christianity began its
course.   One of the most striking points of resemblance is
found in the ruinous and falling condition of the great false
systems which have been the dungeons of the human intellect and heart.   The whole world manifestly feels again to
its centre, and in its entire frame, the omnipotent influence
which moved it in that age

> "Wherein the Prince of light
>   His reign of peace upon the earth began."

The superstitions of Paganism, of Mohammedanism, and
also of the Roman, Greek, Armenian, Abyssinian and other
corrupted forms of the Church, are all kindred of the same
blood not far removed.   The idols, and temples and utensils,
of all of them are decayed ; their priesthoods are anxiously
looking forth to discover the meaning of the signs which in-
dicate that their power over the minds of men is gone, and
that a new spirit is breathed over the face of the earth, the
precursor of the approaching sunrise.*

* We might adopt again, as most truthfully and fully appropriate
to every one of these systems, the pictures of Milton's grand Christ-
mas Hymn.

> " The oracles are dumb,
>   No voice or hideous hum,
>   Runs through the archèd roof in words deceiving ;

There is a particular "mystery of iniquity" whose head "as God sitteth in the temple of God, showing himself that he is God," and who now "letteth, until he be taken out of the way."* What is its condition? The screeching locomotives of the dépôt of the railway, which Gregory XVI. in vain tried to shut out of Rome, confuse the quiet of a Carthusian monastery and the masses in a church beautified by Michel Angelo. The smoke of the gas-works, which

> Apollo from his shrine,
> Can no more divine,
> With hollow shriek the steep of Delphos leaving;
> No nightly trance, or breathèd spell,
> Inspires the pale-eyed priests from the prophetic cell.

> "The lonely mountains o'er,
> And the resounding shore,
> A voice of weeping heard, and loud lament;
> From haunted spring and dale,
> Edgèd with poplar pale,
> The parting genius is with sighing sent;
> With flower-inwoven tresses torn,
> The nymphs in twilight shade of tangled thickets mourn.

> "In consecrated earth,
> And on the holy hearth,
> The lares, and lemures, moan with midnight plaint;
> In urns, and altars round,
> A drear and dying sound,
> Affrights the flamens at their service quaint;
> And the chill marble seems to sweat,
> While each peculiar Power foregoes his wonted seat."

* 2 Thess. ii. 3–11.

now furnish good modern light to the city, is blown by a west wind right across the remains of the palaces of the Cæsars and of the Coliseum, around which hang so many pagan and papal legends. Comic newspapers, filled with ridiculous pictures and stories of the pope and priesthood, are for sale everywhere in the streets. And, best of all, the pope can look down from the high windows of the Vatican upon houses in which those Scriptures in the common tongue are sold, and those Protestant schools taught, which are surely and rapidly undermining the foundations of all his power, and will level it with the dust. Nor can it be long, if rated by the progress of the last few years, until the conclusive changes come. The armies of the truth then should be fully prepared with the financial means instantly to spread the truth amidst all the disorganized dominions of error, and to make known to them the gospel of the Lord Jesus Christ. This necessitates the adoption of a competent system, that which God has provided, in order to furnish those means.

Insufficiency of the American Voluntary System.

The almost universal sentiment of Christians in America is, that the past impulsive, unregulated and partial means of collecting money for ecclesiastical purposes is inadequate to meet the immensely greater demands which the necessities of our land and the evangelization of the world are laying upon us. And these are necessities which, instead of diminishing, are every year becoming greater, and thus rendering our present condition more painful and hopeless.

The European nations have watched and studied our experiment, but have only seen reason to follow in our footsteps so far as they were necessarily compelled to do it. It might have been supposed that the natural sympathies of the Free Church of Scotland with the Presbyterian Church of this country, when it realized the impossibility of uniting temporal maintenance by the State with spiritual independence of the State, and separated from the Establishment, would have led it to adopt our Voluntaryism. But its leaders in the most emphatic language resisted some efforts in that direction. They argued that it is the duty of a Christian government to provide means for the religious and moral education of the poor and vicious; that Voluntaryism was unsuccessful "in making head against the fearfully increased heathenism, and increasing still, that accumulates at so fast a rate throughout the great bulk and body of the common people;" that it did not "reclaim the wastes of ignorance and irreligion and profligacy;" that the congregational selfishness which predominates everywhere "cannot be prevailed on to make large sacrifices for the Christian good of the general population;" and that the spirit was "the spirit of contention," of "demagogism," and of "impatience of restraint." These arguments they supported by statements from the experience of churches in Great Britain and in America. They declared themselves in favor of "an Establishment, but a *pure* Establishment."*

This is the judgment of those who have looked upon our experiments of evangelism from without. They have certainly, while more advantageous to Christianity than exist-

* HANNA; *Life and Writings of Dr. Chalmers*, vol. iv.; and essays by HUGH MILLER and others.

ing Establishments, "failed to reach the lapsed masses." Great districts in our large cities are yielding annually to the advances of practical heathenism. Vast regions of our country are almost entirely destitute of good and efficacious religious influences. The chronic impotency and groans of religious boards and societies of all denominations of Christians may, and should, fill a thinking Christian with both distress and anxiety. The comfort of the churches, the miserable and unrelieved condition of millions in our land, the threatening dangers of Romanism and infidelity, the exceeding littleness of our contributions for the kingdom of Christ on earth compared with our immense expenditures for folly and vices and warfare, all demand, in tones that seem to ring from the judgment-seat of a Righteous God, that we should search the Scriptures and find whether God has not taught his Church some method for a great pecuniary Reformation.

THE PROMISED POWER FROM ON HIGH INDICATES TO THE CHURCH THE WANT OF FINANCIAL MACHINERY SUITED TO IT.

The grand ultimate hope of the Christian Dispensation is "the latter rain" of the Holy Ghost, the descent of the influences from above which are to water the seed of the Gospel sown in the world, and "make the wilderness and the solitary place glad, and the desert rejoice and blossom as the rose."* Most glorious hope of this desolate world! This will indeed "create new heavens and a new earth."

How are those infinitely gracious promises to be realized?

* Isaiah xxxv. and lxv.

There are many who imagine that prayer alone is necessary; or who at least act as if on their part they had nothing to do but to pray. But for such expectations and conduct they certainly have no warrant from what God reveals of his plans and our duties. He makes the express compact: "Bring ye all the tithes into the storehouse, and prove me therewith, if I will not open the windows of heaven and pour you out a blessing." There is not a promise of any one blessing in all the word of God, to saint or sinner, which is not founded upon the condition of his faithful employment of *regular appointed means* to obtain it. It is part of the eternal purpose of good to develop the faculties, capabilities and resources which God entrusts to him.

The Church must make it her chief *business* to advance the earthly kingdom of her Lord. Her order and membership are often spoken of as a grand machinery. The Holy Spirit is the fire. But fire is of no avail unless the machinery be sound and in place, and the different departments be properly attended to; then it will accomplish all the grand results for which engine and machinery were designed. If parts be wanting or defective, if the attendants be ignorant or negligent, then the fire assuredly will die out without effect, or else it will burn or explode the structure. Now a revival of religion in the Church is simply a bestowment of "power." The beneficial or opposite character of its results must depend upon how men perform their part in applying the power to hallowed ends. The gifts of any power may be an injury instead of a benefit. Even miraculous gifts were bestowed upon some unbelievers and men that were lost. The calculation, the economy, the fidelity, of men in employments for their own advantage must be awakened and put in action to accomplish the salvation of a world, in which the mighty influences of the Holy Ghost are even now beginning to be felt.

The apostles were authorized by the circumstances of the age in which they lived to distinguish it by the world-wide proclamation, "Behold, now is the accepted time; behold, now is the day of salvation!"* Thus we may say of the present, *Now* is the era when all are again called "to receive not the grace of God in vain," and to be "*workers with him*," as the apostles besought the Corinthian Church. To be such workers "every one" must give his help, "as God hath prospered him," to increase, train, send abroad and sustain the men, and abundantly supply all instrumentalities which are needed to "preach the gospel to every creature."

THE NEAR APPROACH OF CHRIST'S KINGDOM NECESSITATES OBEDIENCE TO GOD'S RULE OF GIVING TO MEET ITS WANTS.

The coming of Jesus Christ to make atonement for sin was preceded by a grand direct preparation for it among all nations. The Greek empire had already planted its civilization in the great centres of ancient power over the world, and had communicated to them the language in which it was the Divine purpose to give to mankind the New Testament—that book which was to contain the final and complete revelations of his will as to our race until the millennium. The Roman empire was contemporaneous with the coming of Christ. The Romans were law-makers and road-

* 2 Cor. vi. 1, 2; 1 Cor. xvi. 2.

builders. This was their grand mission. As the personal teaching of John the Baptist was the preparation for the teaching of Jesus Christ, so was the spread of Roman influence the preparation for the spread of the gospel of salvation to all the world.

The roads which Rome built were the greatest and most useful monuments of her vast power. They were constructed with far greater outlays of labor and expense than anything of the kind in modern ages. The prophecies of Isaiah were literally fulfilled as to the leveling of mountains and valleys, the straightening of crooked ways, and the making of the rough ways smooth.* Some of those magnificent highways are among the wonders of the world until this day, and have gone for centuries together without repair. Their vast excavations and embankments, their paved bridges, and the care with which they were built in four successive courses of stones of various sizes, solidified with lime, and the surface covered over with blocks of smoothed granite or other hard rock, fitted and jointed like our masonry of walls, have been unparalleled in any subsequent age. They were felt to be the best exhibition, and most needful agency, of Roman superiority. And so they were as speedily as possible constructed over conquered countries. In the Forum at Rome stood a gilded column † inscribed with the names of the principal

---

* Isa. xi. 3–5, and Luke iii. 4–7.

† The location of the *milliarium aureum* is still pointed out by the guides at Rome. It is just at the west end of the *rostra,* or tribune, and was the ideal centre of the city. Under its shadow were delivered many of the speeches of the great Roman orators. Just north of it was the capitol. Near it on the east was the Mamertine prison,

7

roads and the distances to the chief cities upon the course of each of them. They were marked by milestones, frequent stone horse-blocks and other conveniences, and buildings for military and postal necessities. There were taverns near them for travelers. They stretched from one extreme of the empire to the other. Their remains are seen to-day from Scotland, where the gospel was early planted, in the West, to Palestine, whence its preachers started forth with the power of the Holy Ghost, in the East.

The coming of the kingdom and glory of the Lord Jesus Christ beholds in the present day a similar swift and mighty preparation. So urgent and vast is it that this one generation in which we live has seen the grand railroad systems, which now encompass the world ten times as completely as ever did the old Roman roads, invented and perfected and stretched over every continent. It has besides seen almost every ocean and sea covered with large and splendidly furnished vessels propelled by steam. Tens of thousands of miles of postal agencies, incomparably more perfect, useful and cheap than any that Rome every imagined, link together the families and social interests of mankind. And the globe is belted by cords, operated by the lightning of heaven, which instantly flash from the most distant East to

in which it is said the apostles Peter and Paul, and other Christians, were at times confined—a dark and dreadful place, cut out of the solid volcanic rock, and memorable also in the bloody political history of Rome, but in which is a strange, deep, still fountain whose waters are cool and sweet, another "Siloam, which is by interpretation Sent" (John ix. 7), a true symbol of the gospel and its sources of comfort to mankind.

the farthest West the great events of every nation ; a final preparation for the announcement to all mankind of those connected with "the coming of the Son of Man." *

This is a final and most inspiring argument, which can be realized by every one in this day and nation, for the speedy establishment of a financial system which shall accord with the wants of the kingdom of Christ.   It has never yet been done.   God has given us the Rule.   The time calls for its application without delay.   "The kingdom of heaven is at hand !"

* Matt. xxiv. 27.

CHAPTER II.

THE PROGRESSIVE REVELATION OF GOD'S WILL AS TO CHRISTIAN GIVING.

THE gradual development of doctrine in the New Testament, or in the entire word of God, is one of the features of revelation to which the attention of Christian scholars has been strongly directed of late years, and upon which a flood of new light has been thrown.

The Scriptures contain no complete systematic statements as to the moral government of God in heaven, or of that upon earth; as to the structure of the stars, or of the kingdom of nature in this globe; as to the history of mankind; as to prophecy; as to the plan of redemption; or as to Christian duties.

The great field of revelation has been divided into three parts; which are found in the patriarchal dispensation, the dispensation of the law, and the dispensation of the gospel. The great principles which relate to the incarnation, atonement and reign of the Lord Jesus Christ are opened up to man in three different forms or stages: first, occasionally, and but as to their elementary ideas; second, minutely, specifically, and with temporal rewards and penalties attached to them; third, in a broader, less definite, and but more spiritual form, based upon love to God and to the souls of men.

100

In such a way is taught the fact that God designed that an atonement should be made for sin by the shedding of the blood of the Divine Son. First we discern with some difficulty that sacrifices were instituted when Adam was cast out of the garden of innocence; then, next, the law particularizes all their numerous forms, as types of Christ's suffering; then, lastly, Christ dies and rises again from the dead, and the former precise and severe forms are broken up, to advance the Church of a risen Redeemer beyond their pupilage, that it may serve him with more spiritual fidelity, and from deeper, more powerful, and everlasting motives of love and gratitude.

In the same way is unfolded the obligation of the observance of one day in seven as a Sabbath of holy rest and worship. First, we see God resting from the creation of the world on the seventh day, and several allusions to periodic worship in commemoration of it; yet we do not see the word "Sabbath" occur, nor do we read one precept regarding it in all the history of the patriarchal ages down to the giving of the law at Sinai. Under the law, it is most rigidly and solemnly defined; its number is set as a seal upon every division of time—on days, months, years and seven times seven years; and the violation of it is made punishable with death. Finally, in Christ's resurrection from the dead on that day, a new and spiritual seal is set upon the Sabbath; and it becomes joyful and glorious as the pledge, by the risen Creator and Redeemer of mankind, of the fulfillment of the promises of comfort, sanctification and happiness to the soul, the earnest of a reign of peace on earth, and the sign of an eternal rest in heaven.

Just so it is with the ordinance as to property. The same reasons which govern the method in which other important religious truth is revealed will be applicable to the revelation of this. Like the atonement of Christ, which is the basis of the salvation of man, and like the Sabbath, which is the sign and seal of it to the Church, so the ordinance as to offerings of money, which are the chief means by which the army of salvation is to be sent forth and supported in the subjugation of the world, is revealed in three successive forms or stages. First, in the patriarchal age, we distinguish but occasional and brief references to it—a mysterious royal priest, a type of Christ, receives tithes from Abraham; or a Jacob vows a tenth of all that the Lord shall give him as a memorial of the covenant made at Bethel. Then, second, under the law, the ordinances as to tithes and gifts are most minutely specified, applied to the various sources of income, and severe penalties are attached to neglect of payment, even to the extent of excommunication or death. Finally, in Christ, the new and spiritual motives of love and gratitude are planted at the foundation of the duty; a mighty pressure is laid upon the followers of God for greatly enlarged beneficence in the command to preach the Gospel to every creature; and, in view of the vastly multiplied wealth which it was the purpose of God to bestow on Christian nations and people, a greater measure of liberality is enjoined, in the duty that every one shall lay by a weekly apportionment of his income, and also in the designation of the standard of reckoning it, which is to be "as the Lord hath prospered."

It is most important for us thoroughly to study and comprehend the relationship of the leading features of the three dispensations. Moses came not to destroy, but to fulfill, the first rudiments and principles of revelation made to the patriarchs. And Christ came not to destroy, but to fulfill, the fuller and clearer revelations of the law. Each takes the prior foundations; he builds another story of the same house; the fundamental principles of each former dispensation are applied in a more enlarged, spiritual and effectual way. Thus Paul reasons often, for instance, in the verses relating to the support of the ministry. "For it is written in the law of Moses, Thou shalt not muzzle the mouth of the ox that treadeth out the corn. Does God take care for oxen? Or saith he it altogether for our sakes?" etc. Here the law of nature, the law of the old dispensation, and the principles of the gospel, are presented as the root, the stem and the fruit of the same one plant. And he compares them in the same chapter to the consecutiveness of ploughing and threshing, sowing and reaping in the same field.*

The New Testament revelation is in itself progressive as to the duty of giving money for the kingdom of Christ. First we are instructed, in the gospels, as to elementary principles presented in the life, the death and the mission of "Jesus Christ the Son of God;" next, in the Acts, as to the illustrations of them in the spirit, labors and success of the first preachers of the gospel; then by the exposition, in the epistle to the Romans, of the nature of justification by faith in Christ, and its relation to a life of complete holiness and consecration to him; and this brings us to the epistles to the Corinthians, which are explanatory of the

* 1 Cor. ix.

ordinances of the Christian Church.   As the gospels end
with the command to preach the gospel to all the world ; as
the Acts end with the labors of Paul at the world's centre of
power in Rome ; and as the epistle to the Roman Christians
ends with exhortations based upon the assurance of the universal triumphs of the gospel ; so does this epistle to the Corinthians follow up all the teachings as to the ordinances of
the Church with this definite and practical one as to the
pecuniary means by which its heavenly benefits are to be
conveyed and distributed, through human channels and instrumentalities, among all nations.   And this statement of
the rule is followed by varied warnings and encouragements
to this great end in other epistles and in the book of Revelations, which are a sequel to it.   The whole volume closes
with the terrible pictures by John of the final judgment of
antichristian powers and of mankind, and the glorious and
rapturous ones of the millennium and of heaven.   In the
final state of joy they that have been faithful unto death
receive a crown of life.   The gifts and offerings out of the
self-denials of earth are recompensed with an eternal home
in that city whose foundations are garnished with all manner
of precious stones ; and the twelve gates are twelve pearls ;
and the city is of pure gold, as it were transparent glass ;
and the glory of God doth lighten it, and the Lamb is the
light thereof.*

The particular design of this epistle as a corporate part of
the New Testament was to give instruction in regard to the
ordinances of the Church.   It treats of the functions of its
ministry and officers; the impropriety of some customs

* Rev. xxi.

which heathen converts had introduced into public worship; the nature of public prayer; the form of the sacrament of the Lord's Supper; the ground of these ordinances, the resurrection of Christ and of the dead; and finally the proper method of making pecuniary contributions. It is the concluding purpose of the apostle to found the exhortation to Christian zeal, industry and liberality, which we are considering, directly upon the certainty of our resurrection, and the trial and recompenses of the Judgment Day. It was this topic, above all others, which then was the staple of the preaching, the hymns, the prayers, the communion exercises, of the Sabbath day. The resurrection and judgment was the one upon which the apostle would most naturally and powerfully base the instruction and rule in respect to the appropriation and use of money, which is the recompense of all ordinary employments, and the instrumentality of support for the heralds of the gospel.

The formula itself, like the decalogue, the Lord's prayer, and the last command of Christ, is wonderfully concise. One of the evidences of the divine origin, wisdom and authority of a rule which is designed for the instruction of the universal Christian Church in respect to the collection of money for all its diverse and incalculable wants, is the brevity and simplicity of it. The complete summary of universal and perpetual moral law for mankind was given through Moses from Mount Sinai in ten statements, containing but a hundred and fifty-eight words. The perfect model for Christian prayer was stated by Jesus Christ to his disciples in seven sentences of seventy-three words. This ordinance as to Christian stewardship in property was written by Paul in one sentence of thirteen, which our common translation renders in twenty-two words, as follows:

"UPON THE FIRST DAY OF THE WEEK LET EVERY ONE OF YOU LAY BY HIM IN STORE AS GOD HATH PROSPERED HIM."

The most consummate financier in modern ages can add nothing to, and take nothing from, this brief rule. It contains every important principle necessary to the accomplishment of the great end in view. All that is needed is simple obedience to it, in order to fill the treasuries of the Christian Church, to secure for the Church that favor of God which follows from conformity to his will, and to supply means sufficient to send the Gospel to every creature. It is suited to be a complete, abiding and universal rule. It is one which should be put upon the walls of every house of worship; which should be written in the memory and heart of every professor of religion; and which should be taught to every child that has been consecrated to God in Christian baptism.

EXAMINATION OF THE FORM OF THE RULE.

An examination of the form of the rule which is given by the apostle shows its design to be, that Christians should practice a method of appropriating to religious objects a share of the proceeds of all their ordinary labor, which should have some regularity both as to time and amount. Let us first observe the context.

Paul has been teaching, through the Spirit of God, the glorious and wonderful doctrine of the resurrection of the dead. He thus continues, in showing the necessary fruits of it in their life: "Therefore, my beloved brethren, be ye steadfast, unmovable, always abounding in the work of the Lord, forasmuch as your labor is not in vain in the Lord. Now concerning the collection for the saints, as I have given order to the churches of Galatia, even so do ye. Upon the first day of the week let every one of you lay by him in store, as God hath prospered him, that there be no gatherings when I come. And when I come, whomsoever ye shall approve by your letters, them will I send to bring your liberality to Jerusalem." The latter verses of this passage are in our common English version entirely too much dissevered from the first. It must be remembered that the division into chapters has only existed about six hundred years. The direct connection of duty with doctrine is presented, as the inspired writer designed, by our reading the epistle continuously. So Theophylact * and others of the early fathers represent it: "The apostle, having finished the subject of doctrines and now proceeding to treat of moral duties and virtues, leaves the rest and enters upon that of *the queen of virtues*, almsgiving."

That the inspired writer designs this to be an authoritative and general ordinance is evident, in the first place, from its doctrinal connection.

The rule is introduced by a Greek adverb † translated "now." It is more properly *and*, as it is "continuative;" that is, it takes up and carries on a thought which had been interrupted, or "marks something added by way of explanation, example, etc."‡ In this light it should be kept ever before us. The day of the resurrection and judgment

* Quoted by BLOOMFIELD ; *Recensio Synoptica.*   † δέ.

‡ ROBINSON ; *Gr. Lexicon of New Testament.*

approaches to all of us. Let us always "abound in the work of the Lord," in efforts to save souls which with us shall give their account upon that day, knowing that our "labor is not in vain in the Lord," but that "God will render to every man according to his deeds." "*And*" in contributions of money, which are so necessary for the spread of the gospel and benevolent efforts, according to the rule or order which God has given, "even so do ;" that thus we may give with sufficient liberality and the right aims, and that God's blessing may follow the objects for which our money is expended.

Then it is manifest, when we consider the persons addressed, that the object is to establish a positive and general rule. The subject of contributions is one of the chief themes in Paul's two epistles to the Corinthians. The Asiatics of Galatia and other churches in Asia Minor, and the Greeks of Corinth, received the same instructions. There were embraced in them both gentiles and Jews. As new converts they evidently needed clear and positive injunctions on many points. This "order" is the peremptory topic of the closing chapter; a special application, suited to all the Christian churches, of the Redeemer's "last command."

It is sometimes affirmed that the rule was given to the Corinthians and Galatians alone. But it is an extraordinary claim to make, that a wise and important ordinance should be given to one locality; and its benefits or its obligations not be shared in by all others. This is not done with other appointments or admonitions. What is addressed by inspiration to Christians at Colosse, or at Rome, or at Ephesus, every believer unhesitatingly recognizes as intended for all.* Why so scrupulous in this particular matter? Surely every element of claim upon the purse, or upon the self-denial, of a Corinthian or Galatian exists in respect to the duty of professed Christians elsewhere!

The apostle addresses "every one" of them. So that he is laying upon the Corinthians simply the same obligations which belong to all classes of mankind; whether they be in one nation or another; the rich or the poor, the great or the humble, the male or the female members.

A third consideration is that the ordinance was not intended to meet any temporary emergency of the churches of Galatia and Corinth. It was in its nature a general ordinance to the Christian Church; as fully calculated to be universal and perpetual as were the previous ordinances regarding marriage, or the Lord's Supper, or the support of the Christian ministry. This indeed was to be the divine New Testament provision as to the means of the support of the ministry, the functions of whose office the apostle has been so largely discussing in these epistles to the Corinthians. For the want of obedience to this provision of God the Church has suffered, and the world has suffered, beyond all conception. Religion has either been humiliated by her

---

* Thus, says CHRYSOSTOM, to the Corinthians he proposes the example of the Galatians; to the Macedonians the example of the Corinthians; to the Romans that of the Corinthians and Macedonians.—2 Cor. ix. 2. Rom. xv. 26. And he called attention to the consideration that the "Galatians" were not the inhabitants of one city, but of a large province. *Homilies* on 1 Cor.

obligations to the ungodly civil powers, or else by her wants and helplessness.

It is a consideration of weight in regard to the language of the apostle, that the word "collection" in the original* is not a classical, or heathen, Greek word. It signifies a transaction which requires reckoning, consideration, judgment. It is something which Christians everywhere should make a duty and a habit. It has been remarked that "the entire form of the introduction, as well as the article '*the*' before the Greek word translated '*collection*,' indicates that he had spoken before in regard to the matter, and the Corinthians had now, perhaps, inquired how they were to carry it forward."† This is also the meaning of the instruction that he is "to lay aside" money for charitable objects. It is to be a regular *business* of the Christian life of "every one."

The binding and universal character of the ordinance is impressed upon us by a fourth evidence, that of the selection of the verb used in respect to the appointment: "I *have given order*."‡ It is a very strong one. It is the same verb in the original which describes the charge of the Lord Jesus to the twelve apostles. "When Jesus had made an end of *commanding* his disciples." It occurs four other times in the gospels; three times with reference to Christ, and once to the law of the Roman empire. When Christ healed Jairus' daughter, he "*commanded* them to give her meat." He spoke with authority because

---

* λογία, from the root λέγω.

† C. F. KLING, in *Lange's Com.*

‡ διέταξα.

they had "laughed him to scorn." Again, it is used twice when enforcing upon the disciples the necessity of submission to himself. "Doth he [the master] thank that servant because he did the things which *were commanded* him? I trow not. So likewise ye, when ye have done all those things which *are commanded* you, say, We are unprofitable servants." John the Baptist employs it concerning the Roman law, "Exact no more than that which *is appointed* you." In other portions of the New Testament the word is used as a verb or noun in the same sense. Thus, of civil power: "Whosoever resisteth the power, resisteth *the ordinance* of God." It cannot be questioned that the apostle Paul designed the rule he was about to lay down to be a special, authoritative, binding ordinance of a penal nature in the Church, and to be a ground of judgment before the bar of God. He employs the verb of the original four times in this epistle. As to matters relating to divorces: "So *ordain* I in all the churches." As to ministerial support: "Even so *hath* the Lord *ordained*, that they which preach the gospel should live of the gospel." As to the Lord's Supper: "And the rest will I *set in order* when I come." And in the ordinance as to giving, which is before us: "Concerning the collection for the churches, as I *have given order* to the churches of Galatia, even so do ye." These all are "ordinances" binding upon the Christian Church at large. Each has its penalties and its rewards— if indeed we can attach the idea of reward to that which is of the nature of law, and duty, and where it is all of "grace" that we stand and have hope of the glory of God. Then it is of vital importance to each of us that we do not fail in keeping *this* one, and lose the great blessings of obedience, or reap the punishment of neglect.

Finally, the effect of the rule, "that there be no gatherings when I come," is worthy of thoughtful consideration.

Having compendiously and clearly stated the rule, the apostle adds in this brief sentence the reason for his laying it down. He was determined that no extraordinary gatherings in money should be made during his visit to Corinth. The great wisdom of this course is discerned when we observe the character of the people, the condition of the Church, and the objects he had in view. The second epistle, written perhaps a year subsequently, contains numerous references to the rule and throws much light upon its workings. We learn that among his objects were these important ones: to prevent ecclesiastical constraint in giving; to check giving from temporary impulse; to inspire Christians to give in due measure; and to remove grounds for wrong imputations as to the motives of the ministry and officers of the church. These are objections and obstacles which the ministry encounter everywhere, and always must continue to meet, especially in new fields of labor, where their motives are not understood, and they are personal strangers to the people. Indeed under all circumstances of the Church it is most important to detach collections of money from personal considerations connected with the agents who present claims for them, and to make them a matter of conscience before God.

The conclusion to which a thorough examination of the form of this rule, and the part of Scripture immediately related to it, leads us is: that the inspired writer intended to lay down a final ordinance, authoritative and perpetual, like those upon other points of church order and discipline, and peculiarly important to the growth and power of the Church amidst the gentile nations of the earth.

SUMMARY OF INSTRUCTIONS CONTAINED IN THE DIVINE RULE.

We take up this divine rule of the New Testament Church to examine the character of the instructions which it has pleased the great and ever blessed Head of the Church to give for the guidance of its members in this most important matter.

" Upon the first day of the week let every one of you lay by him in store as God hath prospered him."

We easily separate the leading points into four heads. Christian giving is

I. A weekly religious duty;

II. Of universal obligation;

III. By acts of personal consecration and donation;

IV. According to some definite and, with the blessing of God, enlarging proportion of the income.

Let us make it our chief effort and prayer, as Christians, in a matter relating to the service of God and affecting greatly the honor of his Church, to obtain light upon it from the great sources which he has given us, in the teaching of the New Testament, in the preparatory and typical appointments of the Old Testament, and in the interpretations which the Christians of the earliest, and on the whole the brightest, centuries of the Church put upon them.

8

CHAPTER III.

THE SPIRIT OF A PRIMITIVE CHRISTIAN SAB-
BATH: ITS WORSHIP AND INSTRUCTIONS.

OUR FIRST great topic, the command that Christian giving shall be made "ON THE FIRST DAY OF THE WEEK"
—that is, *a weekly religious duty*—opens before us the grand
motives and the occasion of it. If these motives can be
made plain to the Christian mind, and this occasion shown
to be divinely appointed and to be practically the wisest and
most efficient arrangement possible for the end in view, the
most important purpose of this volume will be accomplished.

There are two lights in which we may study this appointment. We may consider the power of the *spiritual* motives
and usefulness of the religious opportunities afforded by the
Sabbath, and we may look at the subject in a purely *secular*
aspect. Let us take it up now in the former of these lights,
the spiritual and religious.

THE WORSHIP OF A PRIMITIVE CHRISTIAN SABBATH.

The primitive Christians had one supreme idea of the
Lord's day, that it was a grand and joyful festival. It was
the great animating centre, the warm and vigorous heart of
their religious life. They celebrated it with every suitable
expression of enjoyment and method of communicating enjoyment to others.

114

Let us bring this conception clearly before our minds by contrasting the original Sabbath of the Church with later methods of the observance of the day.

It was not a sensual Sabbath, like that of the corrupted Christian churches. The Roman Church* retains the one most distinguishing element of the primitive Sabbath in her efforts to make it a festival of enjoyment, or, at least, of excitement; but its liveliest element is wanting. The ancient spirituality is lost. The music, the prayers, the entire sentiment, of a Romanist Sabbath are in their essence sensual. They possess enough of the original conception to make them powerfully fascinating. The thrilling music, the passionate liturgies, the sublime architecture, the glowing and splendid paintings, the rich and gorgeous apparel of the priesthood, completely carry away the senses of the multitude. The emotions created are intense. Women faint under their power. Nothing on earth which is of earth so powerfully moves the soul, carries the whole nature captive and inspires love, admiration, zeal, willingness to give, suffer and dare all things for the sake of the religion.

But the effect is to sensualize the nature. The Roman Catholic Sabbath morning makes the Roman Catholic Sabbath afternoon and evening; and that is the time of the finest operas and dramatic entertainments of the week, of

* The same may be said of the other ancient churches with which American readers generally are not so familiar. The Greek Church worship has many points of resemblance to the Roman. The Russians exhibit equal enthusiasm when engaged in it or speaking of it.

the grandest military parades, of "festive" social entertainments, of exciting exhibitions for the multitude, such as
bull-fights and bear-fights and cock-fights, and the wild and
passionate scenes of the numberless resorts and establishments for gambling.   This is the education which benumbs
the spiritual sense of sin, which makes the bandit; or which
suggests an ascetic, that is still also a sensual, remedy, and
makes the monk and the nun.   All the social and political institutions of a people are thus shaped and colored, as a cas-
tle or palace is conformed to the rock or eminence on which
it is built, by the character of this foundation.

Nor was the original Sabbath austere.   When the Swiss
conscience, looking down from the Alpine refuges from
persecution and strongholds of freedom, saw the grossness
and criminality of Romanism laid low by the great uprising
of the sixteenth century, how natural was it for the chaste
Reformed Church and her children in Scotland and England to become severe.   The sternness, the plainness, the
inflexibility, the chilly rigor of an old Presbyterian or Puri-
tan Sabbath, O, how much they have to excuse them when
we consider that they were the girding on of strong and rough
raiment, the grasping of the iron-shod staff and the dull
lantern, and the preparation of nourishing food and strong
cordials by brave men and women who left the dance and the
laughter to go out and save the people who were perishing
in the darkness and storm.

Nor far less was the primitive Sabbath the inane and
placid modern day, displaying itself in pretty feathers and
silks, amused with the harmonies of a musical quartette,
simpering over a pious lecture on science or domestic duties

as a substitute in the pulpit for the thunders of the Almighty or the invitations to dying men from the cross of Calvary, and putting a dollar into the contribution box which represents the efforts of Christendom for the salvation of hundreds of millions of our race from eternal damnation in hell.

No! We have come to the close of this order of things, to another of the revolutionary eras of the world; one like the deluge, like the day of Moses, like the day of Christ. We have reached the time for the reinstatement of the *Christian* Sabbath.

It is of great importance to the Christian Church in this new "fullness of times," that we inform ourselves as to what the *Christian* Sabbath is. We read often of a European "Continental Sabbath," of a "Scottish Sabbath," or of an "American Sabbath." The good or objectionable features of each, its advantages or its perils, are depicted. But there is only one concern to the minds of the sons of God, who believe that "of his own will begat he them with the word of truth," that "the Spirit of truth" "will guide them into all truth," who profess the creed that "the word of God which is contained in the Scriptures of the Old and New Testaments is the only rule to direct us how we may glorify and enjoy him."* What, then, is the scriptural and original Christian Sabbath? What were its spirit, its worship, and its duties?

THE IDEAL TAKEN FROM THE GREAT JEWISH FESTIVALS.

The ideal of the primitive Christian Sabbath was obtained

* Jas. i. 18.   John xvi. 13.   *Shorter Catechism*, Quest. 2.

from the great festivals of the Jews. The great feasts of
the wave offering of the first sheaf, of Pentecost, or the
feast of weeks, and of tabernacles at harvest, all of them
types of blessings procured through a risen Saviour, were
appointed of God for the first day of the week instead of
the seventh; this would suggest what was the purpose of
the Lord as to the day. The Jewish Sabbath had much
that was joyful in it, but much also that was legal and
severe. The Son of God, he who "made the worlds" and
was "the brightness" of "the glory" of the Godhead,
said: "I am the Light of the world." It was an idea fre-
quently expressed by the apostles that the coming of Jesus
Christ into this world of chaos and darkness was like the
voice which at the first said, "Let there be light and there
was light." This thought connected itself with the Divine
worship of the Sabbath when it was changed to the first
day of the week, and was designated "the Lord's day."*
It is one which gave great joy to the hearts of the early disciples. It is found in the few remains of their writings
which yet exist. One of the personal disciples of the apostle John, Ignatius, was born in Syria. The apostle appointed him, in the year 67, pastor of the great missionary
church of Antioch, where he lived forty years until his martyrdom. Ignatius wrote thus in one of his epistles: † "They
who were brought up in these ancient laws came neverthe-
less to newness of hope, no longer observing the Sabbaths,
but keeping the Lord's day—in which our life also is sprung
up by him." He warned them against Jewish ideas of the

---

* Heb. i. 2, 3.   John viii. 12; i. 4.   2 Cor. iv. 6.   Rev. i. 10.

† *Epistle to Magnesians,* ix. and x.

Christian religion. "Lay aside," said he, "the old, and sour, and evil leaven," and be ye changed into the new leaven, which is Jesus Christ. We at once see how from these principles it came to pass that the Christian worship of the Sabbath should copy those chief feasts which we are told the former Israel often kept "with great gladness, and the Levites and the priests praised the Lord day by day, singing with loud instruments to the Lord." After them the worshipers were "sent into their tents glad and merry in heart for the good which the Lord had showed unto his people." They "made them days of feasting and joy and of sending portions one to another and gifts to the poor."* These great festivals were imitated as to their most important features in the Lord's day of the early Christians.

DESCRIPTIONS BY WRITERS OF THAT AGE.

The sore persecutions of the early Christians were like a dark cloud which yet reflected back light to distant places. They were forced to make public defences and explanations of their practices, which are most instructive and precious to us now. Two of these defences were written by Justin Martyr, a Greek by parentage, who was born at Sychar in Samaria, only twenty years after the death of the last apostle, John. He became a Christian and wrote several books, which are yet extant, against idolatry, or explanatory of his religion. In his first Apology, addressed to the emperor Antoninus Pius, he gives an account of the way in which the Christians then kept the Sabbath. He says:

"Those of us who have the means assist all who are in

* 2 Chron. xxx. 21; vii. 10. Esther ix. 22.

want; and in all our oblations we bless the Maker of all
things through his Son, Jesus Christ, and through the Holy
Ghost. On the day which is called Sunday there is an assembly in the same place of all those who live in the cities,
or in the country districts. The records of the apostles, or
the writings of prophets, are read as long as the time will
allow. When the reader concludes, the presiding minister
gives oral instruction. Then we all rise and offer up our
prayers. When we have concluded our prayer, bread is
brought in, and wine and water. The presiding minister
again in the same way offers up prayers and thanksgiving
with his utmost power, and the people express their concur-
rence by saying Amen.

"There is then a distribution and a partaking, by every
one, of the elements used in the supper; and to those who
are not present they are sent by the hands of the deacons.
Those who are in a prosperous condition, and wish to do so,
then give what they will, each according to his judgment.
What is collected is placed in the hands of the presiding
minister; who assists with it orphans and widows, and such
as from sickness or any other cause are in distress; and he
grants aid to those who are in bondage, to strangers from
afar, and, in a word, to all who are in need.

"But Sunday is the day on which we all hold our common assembly, because it is the first day on which God,
when he changed darkness and matter, made the world;
and the same day on which Jesus Christ our Saviour rose
from the dead. For on the day before the (Roman) Saturday
he was crucified, and on the day after it, which is Sunday,
he appeared to his apostles and disciples, and taught them

these things which we have presented to you for your consideration."

To get as clear an idea as possible of a primitive Christian Sabbath, which is most necessary to the object which we have now before us, let us look at the picture of it in another of the ancient Apologies, that of Tertullian, who was born at Carthage within sixty years after the time of the death of the apostle John. He thus describes, in the earliest Christian writings which we have in the Latin language, the worship which the heathen so grossly misrepresented.* "We Christians—united in one body by our common faith, worship and hope—meet for prayer, in which we, as it were, take the kingdom of heaven by a violence grateful to God. . . .

"We assemble also for receiving instruction, warning and exhortation from the Divine word, whereby we nourish our faith, animate our hope, establish our confidence, and stir up ourselves by every argument to the practice of good works. On these occasions discipline is administered with all solemnity, and the censures pronounced on offenders are regarded as anticipating the judgment to come.

"Every one puts something into the public stock once a month, or when he pleases, and according to his ability and inclination, for there is no compulsion; these pious deposits are applied, not to the indulgence of appetite, but in aid of the poor, orphans, the aged, the shipwrecked, the persecuted, and for burying the dead.

"Then follows a supper, a feast of charity, not an entertainment for the sensual, but a refreshment to the hungry and

* *Apologet.,* c. 39.

the needy.   To this supper we do not sit down till we have previously tasted the pleasure of prayer to God; we sup in the recollection that God may be worshiped in the night season, and we converse with the consciousness that he hears us. Praise succeeds, and the whole is concluded with prayer."

In our study of these and other sketches of the primitive Christian Sabbath, which are given more or less in detail, there rise to our mind the prominent features of the worship which was celebrated upon it.

THE JOYFUL CHARACTER OF THE PRIMITIVE WORSHIP.

The chief joy of the day was its fervent devotional exercises.   It was the day which the Lord Jesus hallowed by his successive appearances after his resurrection, when their "hearts burned" with the emotions of his personal communications.   It was the day when amidst their assembly "in one place" the fiery baptism of the Holy Ghost descended,* and they were like "men full of new wine." "We celebrate Sunday," said Tertullian, "as a joyful day. On the Lord's day we think it wrong to fast or to *kneel* in prayer."

Let the reader try to conceive of the sensations of a new

---

* OLSHAUSEN, on Acts ii. 1, says: "As the Church has quite rightly fixed the day of the Redeemer's death upon Friday, although the Passover began ou Thursday evening at six o'clock, so also has it with equal propriety fixed the first Pentecost upon the day which occurred exactly seven weeks after the resurrection. . . . Undoubtedly the Jewish Pentecost in the year of our Lord's death began at six o'clock in the evening when the Sabbath was at a close, and it lasted until six o'clock on Sunday evening."

convert from heathenism who first realizes the indescribable greatness, and glory, and happiness of the revelation that there is *one* "true God, the living God, and an everlasting King," and that he is permitted to call him "*my* God," "which keepeth covenant and mercy with them that love him." Then he may be prepared to celebrate like the first Christians that glorious act of creation, of which the Sabbath is the everlasting memorial, which caused the angelic witnesses, "the morning stars," to sing together, and the sons of God to shout for joy.* Then may he realize the happiness of those who, even amidst hunger and nakedness and in tribulation, lovingly trust day by day for "daily bread" to their "Father in heaven." The "hallelujahs" of the closing psalms of David or Ezra will inspire him with a rapture which he never before knew.

> "Praise ye him, all his angels !
> Praise ye him, all his hosts !
> Praise ye him, sun and moon !
> Praise him, all ye stars of light !"

> "Kings of the earth, and all people ;
> Princes, and all judges of the earth !
> Both young men, and maidens ;
> Old men, and children !"

> "Let everything that hath breath praise the LORD !
> Praise ye the Lord !"

The Sabbath was above all other employments a day of praise to Christ, the Son of God, the Messiah, who "made peace through the blood of his cross," the risen and ascended King and Head of "things in earth and things in

* Job xxxviii. 7.   Deut. vii. 9.   Jer. x. 10.

heaven." "The word of Christ dwelt in them richly, in all wisdom; teaching and admonishing one another in psalms and hymns and spiritual songs; singing with grace in their hearts to the LORD."*

The heathen noticed this distinguishing worship. The philosopher Pliny† described the Christians as those who "affirmed that the whole of their fault or error lay in this, that they were wont to meet together on a stated day, before it was light, and sing among themselves by turns a hymn to Christ as God." The following verses are a translation of part of a hymn, the earliest we possess, which is found in the writings of Clement of Alexandria:

"Shepherd of tender youth,
    Guiding in love and truth,
        Through devious ways;
    Christ our triumphant King!
    We come thy name to sing,
    And here our children bring,
        To shout thy praise.

"Ever be thou our Guide,
    Our Shepherd and our pride,
        Our staff and song!
    Jesus! thou Christ of God!
    By the perennial word,
    Lead us where thou hast trod,
        Make our faith strong.

"So now, and till we die,
    Sound we thy praise on high,
        And joyful sing.

* Col. i. 12–20; iii. 16.

† Letter to Trajan.

Infants, and the glad throng,
Who to thy Church belong,
Unite and swell the song
To Christ our King !"

Joyful singing and praise should certainly occupy a much larger share of our Sabbath worship. The fervent Moravians and other German Protestants sometimes accompany it not alone with the organ, but also with trumpets and brass instruments, which impart a peculiarly melodious and inspiring effect.

Christ has said, "As my Father *hath* sent me, so *send* I you."* Every Christian therefore felt himself and herself to be "a missionary," one *sent* and delegated to help in some way to save a lost world! The Sabbath then was a day of ardent prayer for missionary success, and of triumph on account of the mighty victories which were continually announced through the outpouring of the Holy Ghost upon city after city, and nation after nation ; following to the distant West and East the Roman arms with conquests infinitely more beneficial to the world, which caused joy to the angels that are in heaven.

The Sabbath was, upon the faith of God's covenant and word, regarded as a sacred pledge of a millennium on earth and rest in heaven to the bodies and spirits of the faithful —the coming "rests" and "sabbatisms."† The very ancient epistle attributed by many to Barnabas says‡ that "in six days—that is, in six thousand years—shall all things be

* John x. 21.
† Heb. iv. 9.   Rev. xix. 16.   Rom. viii. 21.
‡ *Cath. Epist.* xv.

accomplished. And what is this that he saith, 'And he rested the seventh day?' He meaneth this, that when his Son shall come, and abolish the season of the wicked one, and judge the ungodly; and shall change the sun, and the moon, and the stars; then he shall gloriously rest on that seventh day." Their ideas of the dates of these great events were uncertain and even contradictory; but of this they were certain, and in this they triumphed, that Jesus Christ should be "KING OF KINGS AND LORD OF LORDS," and that the creation "shall be delivered from the bondage of corruption into the glorious liberty of the children of God."

If the Sabbatic memorials and hopes so greatly animated the prayer, and praises, and songs of the primitive Christians, how much more should they swell with joy ours, to whom the glories of "the latter day" are so much more near! The wonderful extent to which the science of music has been cultivated by the present generation is one "earnest" of the promise, "my servants shall sing for joy of heart;" "with the voice together shall they sing, when the LORD shall bring again Zion."* We have perfected instruments† of music. We have taught the young children of Christendom to sing. We have gathered the sweetest melodies from every land, many of which before were in the service of the devil.‡ We behold the heavenly power of

* Isa. lxv. 14; lii. 8.

† The piano interests us as the most advanced of the improvements, traceable through the intervening ages, of the original harp of Central and Western Asia.

‡ Not only are some of them from operas and other worldly

sanctified music conquering the debased masses of Scotland and Ireland and England. Just so have we also seen it melt the hearts of the heathen in foreign fields of labor. It will be, when fully made an instrument of the Holy Spirit, a chief one among the mighty means of filling the earth with "the glory of the Lord." Joyful praises are the best way to make God's "will be done on earth as it is done in heaven!"

The Instruction of a Christian Sabbath.

An intelligent heathen who has picked up a historical conception of Christianity out of the gospels distributed by missionaries, in visiting a Christian country, is surprised to observe a great difference between the methods of religious instruction practiced now and those pursued by him whom we claim to be the divine and all-wise Teacher. Let us go back to the New Testament and examine this model. It will enable us to conceive of the methods which his disciples followed, whose labors converted the civilized world to the Christian faith.

Example of Jesus as a Teacher.

Jesus lived and taught like one who had come to deliver a momentously important message to men, wherever he

agencies of pleasure, but some are from the Africans of the South and from the dark races of heathen lands. The palanquin-bearer, or coolie, in India, sometimes surprises the Christian stranger by bursting out with the air of our child's hymn, "I want to be an angel." It is originally that of a Hindustani love-song, the words of which begin thus when translated, "There came a Mogul woman," etc.

could reach them, and to pity and relieve them to the utmost in the little while before he would go away to return thus no more. He paid little respect to localities, to edifices, and to forms; he pursued the lost sheep by the seaside, on the mountains, in the cornfield, amidst the abodes of pain or the haunts of sinners. His sermons were only at times theological in structure; but they expounded largely the written word. Their language was simple as a little child's. He drew illustrations which would interest the common people from all their employments, and fixed the truth in their minds by striking parables. His miracles were lessons, and evidences, by which he addressed also their eyes, their touch, and their wants and appetites. The form of his discourses was most often conversational; like that of the instructions of the other greatest teachers of mankind, as Socrates, Confucius, or Buddha; and he encouraged questions and answers. Their aim was pointed, personal, tending to immediate volition, action and results. He made it a great and essential part of his mission to exhibit specimens of its proper fruit by the side of the seed and the root which he sought to induce men to take and to propagate; therefore it was that he healed the sick, and gave sight to the blind, restored their hearing to the deaf, imparted speech to the dumb, and bestowed food upon the hungry.

Just what Jesus did the apostles and disciples copied. So did also several succeeding generations of Christians. It was *this practical* Christianity, and *this* preaching, which overcame every obstacle to its progress. Is it too much to say that, if it had been persevered in, the gospel would long before this time have overcome all the powers of the world?

The public duties of the Sabbath day were performed at various times of the day. . Pliny says: "They separated and came together again." Those duties which came later clustered about the communion of the Lord's Supper, and the *agapé*, or "feast of charity," and the exercise of the duties connected with them.

It would be a natural thought to Paul, in shaping an epistle to a church, such as that to the Romans, or Ephesians, or Colossians, to conform the order of subjects somewhat to that which was familiar in the exercises of a Christian Sabbath. An epistle of his may thus be to us the representation of such a holy day in the apostolic age. We trace successively in it the abundant prayers and praises, the doctrinal instruction, the practical exhortations, and the closing individual salutations and communications.

EMPLOYMENT OF SUNDAY AFTERNOON AND EVENING.

This brings us to the consideration of a subject which is very important to the Christian Church of this age: What is the proper employment of Sunday afternoon and evening?

To the early Christians this was the most practically delightful part of the day: to Christians now it is the opposite. It is now a repetition of the morning worship. Or it is an hour for "popular" and questionable themes. It is attended with reluctance by great numbers. In some churches the proper membership and families give place almost entirely to strangers. There have been many dis-

9

cussions as to what to do with Sunday afternoon. Some of the most excellent ministers have seriously considered and spoken of the propriety of dropping the second public service, and turning the time to as much advantage as possible in the Sabbath-school, in family religious duties, and in private religious exercises. But God hath provided some better thing for us. "This is the day which the Lord hath made: we will rejoice and be glad in it." * If the founders of our faith are worthy to be accepted as our guides, it is manifest that the Sabbath afternoon and evening are the fitting times for the consideration of the great practical duties of Christianity, and for some measure of performance of them.

APPROPRIATE THEMES.

Our subject at present is the instruction of the Christian Sabbath. Let us suppose a pastor to be thoroughly imbued with the spirit of Jesus Christ and of the apostles and sincerely desirous, for the glory of Christ, for the spread of the gospel in all the world, and for sinning and suffering men's sake, thoroughly to awaken and educate his congregation to pray and work and give ; then how boundless the range and variety of topics suitable, if intelligently and spiritually presented, for Sabbath afternoon exercises. How many are there that he may, with God's help, turn to the most practical "charitable" ends.

1. There are *scripture* themes. The glory of God as the Creator of all. The glory of the kingdom of Christ. The life of Christ on earth. The offices of Christ. The atonement of Christ. The personality, offices, and influences of the

* Ps, cxviii. 24,

Holy Spirit. The three dispensations. The millennium. The providence of God over the human race. The prophecies collectively; in particular books; those referring to different lands; to particular subjects;·modern fulfillment. Missionary influence of Judaism. The ten commandments. The lives and labors of different apostles. Topics of the Lord's Prayer. The Lord's Supper. Baptism. The apostolic commission. Scripture lessons on objects and uses of money. The divine rule for giving. Dangers of covetousness, illustrated from Bible history, etc. The Judgment Day, grounds of trial and final awards.

2. General *ecclesiastical* topics. Church history. Origin and purposes of the several departments of Church work; collateral fields of effort connected with each of them; bearing of each on the great designs of the Redeemer's kingdom; relations of Church courts to raising up laborers and spreading the gospel; duties of members, training and spirit of workers for Christian purposes. Enterprises of other branches of the Christian Church. Consecration and employment of money and property; vital importance of prayer in accomplishment of all good.

3. Various *classes* in the church. Parents. Sabbath and other teachers and schools. Elders. Deacons. Different associations for congregational work. Officers. Duties, privileges, and opportunities of women. Claims of the ministry upon young men. Baptized children. Duties of business men. Responsibilities of professional men, and need of the world for Christian men of each class at home and abroad.

4. *Particular objects* needing co-operation. Character,

circumstances and wants of particular classes of society, or fields, or nations. Claims of temperance societies; total abstinence. Duties toward the suffering; the blind, mutes, imbeciles, the insane; the aged; asylums, reform-schools, poor-houses. Prisoners. Seamen. Religious press. Special emergencies.

5. *Related themes.* Religious ends of various sciences. Christian commerce. Lessons of passing events in the world.

INTEREST OF THE PEOPLE.

To make these meetings more interesting and profitable the assistance and co-operation of the lay members of the Church should be judiciously called in; "if any one hath a psalm, hath a doctrine, hath a tongue, hath a revelation, hath an interpretation: let all things be done unto edifying." The gifts and knowledge of many may be used in some form or other, to the advantage of the church and themselves.

One of the profoundest lessons of our Lord's earthly ministry lay in his treating old and young alike in a method which we, in our pride, folly and want of sympathetic apprehension, set aside except for children. We should arouse and fix attention, add to the information communicated, and excite earnest emotion and practical results, by employing suitable means of illustration—pictures, cards, maps, blackboard sketches, articles of dress and worship and use, and written correspondence. The mind commonly receives twice as distinct impressions if communicated through two senses. The aim should be distinctness, emotion, action, profitable and tangible results.

If thirty years is the average of human life, two thirds of each generation are yet in their minority; they are the most impressible, and the purest and best part of the generation; the part who are coming into action as the rest are going out. It is of immense consequence then to make the Sabbath tell with greatest effect, in all its appointments and efforts, upon that preponderating and most important majority.

HINTS FROM THE MONTHLY CONCERT.

The manner in which the " Monthly Concert of Prayer for Missions" has been observed, when made really effective, affords some profitable hints as to the best way for a church to spend the Sabbath afternoon.

The Monthly Concert has fulfilled its design; a very important one in the initial stage of Christian missions. But it could not be universal or permanent for several reasons. The object was limited—covering but one of the range of Christian and ecclesiastical claims. Sufficient instruction and variety could not be provided for in the exercises. The hour commonly appointed, on a week-day, apparently detached it as an act of worship and duty from the organic and essential work of the church. The persons taking part in it usually were comparatively few in number; and they were not those who most needed to be taught and incited. The young and the indifferent portion of the people were not reached.

The true Sabbath afternoon exercises of a congregation should possess the spirituality, the freedom, the illustrative character, the occasional addresses and prayers from the lay members, the practical tone, the money contributions, of the

Monthly Concert. But it should be the Monthly Concert greatly enlarged in its scope, infused with a life that shall interest and stir every class and age, made far more practical in its aims, lifted into complete communion with all the great aims of the Church, and glorified with a nobler and more joyous worship of Christ.

THE GRAND END OF ALL.

The grand end, to which all else should conform, and by which all the Sabbath services of every kind should be inspired, is the honor of the LORD JESUS CHRIST. One beholds, in approaching an island of the Pacific or Eastern seas, and even while at a great distance from it, the volcanic mountain to which it at first owed its existence. The magnificent gray peak, seamed by its eruptions, stands far above all the clouds. It is supposed to be inhabited by the gods. It is the supreme object of attraction to every eye by day. Its fire, if in action, lights the whole heavens in the night. When the sun becomes hot, the clouds gather round it, without reaching its summit, and form a white and far-spreading umbrella, that shelters the people who live upon its slopes. The sailors, tossed about by the winds and waves, make it the great mark by which to guide their course wherever they go. Now all this, and infinitely more—Omnipotent Creator, Source of all life and joy and comfort, the Guide to our spirits tossed in the storms of life, our King, our God, our All—is JESUS CHRIST. Every duty of the Sabbath of his appointment, should exalt him, and tend to extend the blessings of his reign over the hearts of men. Yes, every act and word and thought of every day also, should be such as become creatures who live by his goodness, mercy and grace; and who must so live for ever and for ever.

THE THREE POWERS THAT WILL CONQUER THE WORLD.

And now, to keep clearly before us the practical ends of this volume, let us remember that the chief ways in which we are to seek to advance the honor of Jesus Christ through all the exercises of the Sabbath are these three: prayer, personal labors and influence, and the giving of money. Prayer moves God's almighty power; the personal labors and influence of men and women are the ordained intelligent agency of God, on earth; money is the great material agency of man. These three must be combined in order to conquer the world for Christ Jesus, the Son of God.

PRAYER.

Prayer,—the sense of need of prayer,—the conviction of the heavenly power of prayer,—the assurance of the glory, and blessedness, and triumphs of prayer,—this is the foundation upon which all our labors, and upon which all our consecration and gifts of money, must be built. It is prayer that moves GOD! All else is in itself but of man. And what is man compared with God? Man moves himself over the surface of the globe like a little mite upon the sides of a great cannon ball, requiring months, or years, to pass around it. But GOD projects this ball, and innumerable millions which are immeasurably greater than it, here and there through the infinite universe, hundreds of millions of miles while man is creeping that little circuit. And just so incomparably, infinitely,

more great than man's, is God's power. He could anni-
hilate, he could build again, the world with a word.. He
could convert all mankind with one smile; or he could send
them all to hell with one frown. He but delays his action,
he but moves slowly through the events of our eras of history, in order patiently to *educate* us for eternity! *"God
so loves"* us!

The chief purpose of this education of the Church is to
teach it *to pray;* that is, to depend upon, and ask, and
bless him, in all its various and numerous wants.

Jesus said, "Therefore pray ye: Hallowed be thy name;
thy kingdom come; thy will be done in earth as it is in
heaven."

"Therefore said he unto them, The harvest truly is great,
but the laborers are few: pray ye therefore the Lord of
the harvest that he would send forth laborers into his
harvest."

"Pray to thy Father which is in secret, and thy Father
which seeth in secret, shall reward thee openly."

"He went out into a mountain to pray, and continued all
night in prayer to God. And when it was day, he called
unto him his disciples; and of them he chose twelve, whom
also he named apostles."

"He went up into a mountain to pray; and as he prayed,
the fashion of his countenance was altered, and his raiment
was white and glistering."

"They all continued with one accord in prayer and supplication." "And suddenly there came a sound from
heaven, as of a rushing mighty wind, and it filled all the
house where they were sitting." "And they were all filled

with the Holy Ghost, and began to speak with other tongues, as the Spirit gave them utterance." "And the same day there were added unto them about three thousand souls." *

PERSONAL LABORS AND INFLUENCE.

What a wondrous chain of celestial promises we have in the following passages! "Since by man came death, by man came also the resurrection of the dead." "Unto the angels hath he not put in subjection the world (or dispensation) to come." "For both he that sanctifieth, and they who are sanctified, are all of one; for which cause he is not ashamed to call them brethren." "Therefore are they before the throne of God, and serve him day and night in his temple; and he that sitteth on the throne shall dwell among them." "And they that be wise shall shine as the brightness of the firmament; and they that turn many to righteousness as the stars for ever and ever." †

THE GIVING OF MONEY.

This is the third of the powers which must be leagued together, in joint and harmonious action, that the whole world may be subdued to the Lord Jesus Christ. God acts through man for the salvation of man. Man, in the universal co-operation of all the membership of the Church to fill the world with the blessings of the gospel, must chiefly act through money. Let us proceed to consider the office of money in the Church.

* Matt. vi. 6, 9. Luke x. 2; vi. 12; ix. 29. Acts i. 14; ii. 2–4, 41.
† 1 Cor. xv. 21. Heb. ii. 5, 11. Rev. vii. 15. Dan. xii. 3.

CHAPTER IV.

THE PRIMITIVE COMMUNION: GIFTS IN WORSHIP.

IT is strange to notice how far, oftentimes, our familiar English words have departed from the original ideas which gave them birth. Thus the word "communion" is now defined, in its application to a part of our religious worship, to be simply a celebration of the Lord's Supper; and the word "sacrament" is but a synonym for the same passive reception, in these days, of consecrated bread and wine, for spiritual nutriment and comfort.

But the ancient Romans, from whom these words came, affixed them to the ceremony with a widely different meaning. Then every city and town was a military camp; every man was a soldier; and every woman and child was glad to help to burnish and keep the sword and shield. Roman legions had conquered the world, and the Christians were determined that the Church of Jesus Christ should also conquer it. These words, found in the ancient ecclesiastical Latin, are among the illustrations of the high and courageous determination. The Latin for "communion" meant at first the "building together," or guarding together, "of a city wall;" and the "sacrament" was the *sacred* "military oath" by which soldiers bound themselves to adhere to, fight and suffer for, their leader and each other. The word "sacrament" had also a legal use. It was the sum of money which was required as a deposit, or pledge, from the parties to a suit; which was put for security in the hands of officers or priests, kept in a *sacred* place, and sometimes forfeited to religious objects.* These radical ideas explain the full Christian sense of the terms referred to. The original state of the Church was that of a body engaged in an unending war. The epistles of the New Testament abound in military metaphors. And also the writings of the early fathers. The Lord's Supper was not a mere "feast." It was an occasion of the taking of a solemn pledge, to their Lord and to each other, and of giving contributions of money and other means which were necessary to plant the standard of the gospel upon all the strongholds of sin, and destroy the dominion of all "the principalities and powers" of hell over the race of man.†

New Testament Meanings of "Communion."

We turn to the Greek of the New Testament, and discover an equal departure at the present time from the original inspired ideas. The word which in English is translated "communion"‡ is from a root which signifies that which is common, public, open to others; and possibly therefore with the sense of its being defiled by that contact. The derivative of which we speak is applied to the Lord's Supper in

---

* These uses of the Latin words are common in the Commentaries of Cæsar, Orations of Cicero, and elsewhere. They can be examined, with references, in the Lexicons of Freund, Andrews, etc.

† Eph. vi. 12. 2 Cor. x. 4.

‡ κοινωνία (*koinōnia*).

a number of successive senses, which it is important for us to examine that we may understand the original ordinance.

The solemn occasion of the establishment of the "communion" is too well known to require comment—the scene in which the Lord Jesus first, like a slave, washed the feet of his disciples, enjoining upon them similar humble willingness to serve one another; then gave to them the emblems of his great and all-sufficient sacrifice in his own blood for all the sins and woes of men, and of their fellowship with him in its spirit and purposes.*

We take up the apostolic observance of it, along with the converts upon whom the Holy Ghost was poured out at, and after, Pentecost. "They continued steadfastly in the apostles' doctrine and *fellowship* (*communion*), and in breaking of bread and in prayers." "And all that believed were together, and had all things *common;* and sold their possessions and goods, and parted them to all men as every man had need. And they, continuing daily with one accord in the temple, and breaking bread from house to house, did eat their meat with gladness and singleness of heart, praising God, and having favor with all the people. And the Lord added to the Church daily such as should be saved." †

The communion of the Lord's Supper was then the central scene of the enjoyment and duties of the Sabbath day. The epistles of the New Testament, and the writings of the primitive Christians, are full of allusions to it. We trace in those of the New Testament two classes of leading ideas; related to the reception, or to the bestowment, of good.

First, there is in *this,* and in some degree in *other* acts

* John xiii., etc.   † Acts ii. 42–47.

of "communion," the joy of the glorious fellowship with God, in each of the persons of the Trinity.   John, the beloved disciple, who lay in the bosom of Christ at the last Supper, and never forgot it, says: "And truly our (*communion*) *fellowship* is with the Father, and with his Son Jesus Christ."   Paul says of the *communion* of the believer with the eternal Godhead, " God is faithful, by whom ye were called into the *fellowship* of his Son Jesus Christ." He cries to the church of Corinth, in this epistle in which there are so many instructions as to the ordinances of the Christian Church, "The cup of blessings which we bless, is it not *the communion* of the blood of Christ?   The bread which we break, is it not *the communion* of the body of Christ?"   And even Peter, that had so many bitter things of shame and of repentance to remember in connection with the *first* communion, wrote "to the strangers scattered " abroad, often by persecution, "Rejoice, inasmuch as ye (*share in communion*) *are partakers of* Christ's sufferings, that, when his glory shall be revealed, ye may be glad also with exceeding joy."   This communion was styled that (*the fellowship*) " of the Spirit."   And the joyful scenes of the Sabbath were closed with the solemn benediction, which invoked the continued grace of the Son, Jesus Christ, the love of the Father and " *the communion* of the Holy Ghost " to " be with " them " all."*

PRACTICAL COMMUNION OF CHRISTIANS.

Next, without dwelling upon them, the uses of the word

* 1 John i. 3.   1 Cor. i. 9; x. 16.   1 Pet. iv. 13.   Phil. ii. 1. 2 Cor. xiii. 14.

"communion" as gathering about the employments and associations on the Sabbath may be studied from various passages. Paul recalls how, when he was recognized as an apostle, "James and Cephas (Peter) and John" "gave me and Barnabas the right hand of (*communion*) fellowship." He writes to the Philippians, "I thank God for your (*communion*) fellowship in the gospel." He warns the vain Corinthians against brotherly associations and family connections with unbelievers; "for what *communion* hath light with darkness?"—"ye are the temple of the living God." John admonishes "the elect lady," "receive not into your house" one who rejects Christ, "neither bid him God speed; for he that biddeth him God speed *is partaker* (as if in a *communion*) of his evil deeds."*

The exercises of the Lord's Supper were followed, either directly or at a later hour of the day, by the "Feast of charity." This was a regular part of the Sabbath employment. It was in accordance with the idea of the Sabbath as a Jewish "festival." It was in the spirit of the commemoration of the resurrection of Christ, and of his teaching, "When thou makest a feast call the poor, the maimed, the lame, the blind, and thou shalt be blessed; for they cannot recompense thee, for thou shalt be recompensed at the resurrection of the just." These feasts gave opportunity for inquiries into the wants of the suffering, for counsels together in regard to charitable efforts and enterprises, and, the early historians tell us, for the reconciliation of differences among themselves. They were also joyful occasions of fraternal religious intercourse. Yet they were not with-

* Gal. ii. 9. Phil. i. 3. 2 Cor. vi. 14–16. 2 John 11.

out some dangers to the Christians; partly from those who misconceived and abused their opportunities and freedom, and became dark "spots" upon them.*

Thus it is evident that the enjoyments and associations of which the Lord's Supper was the centre in the ancient Church made the idea of "communion" a very precious and potent one in the Christian mind.

We must not carry this interpretation too far. We would not infer that the word "communion," in the passages which have been quoted, necessarily implies that all the spirit of piety and works of love to which they refer were connected only with the Lord's Supper, nor, further, that this ordinance is to be celebrated every Sabbath day now. But they do imply that the Lord's Supper, the "Feasts of charity," and the other associated exercises of the ancient Sabbath, were the best type, and the chief source, and the most common occasion of these feelings and works. Or, to go back to the foundation of all, these do spring from the great joy of the fact of which they are the memorial—that Jesus, who was crucified and slain, God hath raised and made to sit on his throne, and that as the divine Head of the Church he bestows all heavenly gifts upon men.

THE ORIENTAL IDEAS OF HONORARY GIFTS.

It often surprises reading people to notice how difficult it appears to be for us to convince the nations of the East that we people of America and Europe are *not* "barbarians." This is argued in state papers; it is insisted upon in friendly discussions of merchants and missionaries. Yet there we

* Luke xiv. 13. Judo 12. 2 Pet. ii. 12.

stand, before those whom we know are far beneath us in
knowledge, in power, and in religious advantages, occupying
the humiliating position of defence in the question whether
we ourselves possess the first elements of civilization. The
Oriental grants that we have a wolfish or serpent-like fac-
ulty of burrowing into the earth, discovering mines of the
metals and coal, and utilizing in the most wonderful way
material substances for selfish and gross ends; and that we
possess demon-like powers of warfare and destruction. He
may discern that we have some stern and severe moral virtues, such as truthfulness and impartiality in the adminis-
tration of justice. And yet he judges us uncivilized. *He*
understands, in our Scriptures, the deep deference and consideration of the seven days' silence of the friends of the
smitten Job; *we* do not. *He* appreciates Mary's kissing
Jesus' feet, and bathing them in tears, and breaking a precious vase of most costly aromatic oil, bought from many a
year's small savings, to anoint them; *we* do not. *He* comprehends that the commission of Babylonish sages or priests
which visited Palestine, to ascertain the locality and circumstances of the birth of the long-expected "King of the
Jews," could not have come thither without a rich and
appropriate oblation of "gold, frankincense, and myrrh;"
we do not. The sentiments, sympathies, forms, and especially the becoming material representations, of profound respect for authority, for age, for superior wisdom, for sanctity, which fill the book which we call *our* Bible, but that is
only *half* ours as to either our understanding or obedience,
all are but natural and customary to him. The substantial
manifestation of professions of affection and honor in suit-

able gifts is with him necessary and indispensable. The people who do not comprehend and practice such usages of the great nations and most ancient homes of mankind in the Old World he looks upon as ignorant, avaricious, rude "barbarians," savages that need to be taught and made to perform the requirements of the respect which is due to fellows or to superiors. Now it is these natural, these sound, these admirable, these ancient and everlasting principles, that underlie as foundations some of the duties which the vagrant character of our ancestry for thousands of years, which our distribution to "the ends of the world," and which the debasing necessities of our laborious colonization and primary cultivation of a new and unknown continent, have caused us to forget.

We cannot understand the Bible, we cannot perform the mutual duties of Christians, we cannot comprehend the appointments of Infinite Wisdom, Majesty and Love, for the guidance of the Church in its plans to regenerate and ennoble our fallen race, until we do thoroughly inquire into the religious significance of gifts. And until the Church, here and everywhere, puts into practice the principles and obligations of Scripture as to regular, frequent, generous and loving gifts, as God hath prospered, and as Christ's kingdom needs for its beneficent purposes, we must continue to witness the same terrible state of darkness and death in the world, the same want of the moving of the Divine Spirit through the moral chaos, though that omnipotent Spirit could in a breath cause all to be glorious with creative light, and the same dominion of hell on earth which has existed for so many ages past.

10

GIFTS OF SABBATH WORSHIP AND COMMUNION.

With some conception of the office and importance of gifts in the Oriental and Scriptural light, we are prepared to recognize their place in the original "communion" of Christians. The material gift is to the Eastern mind the highest expression of sincere love and honor. The grand festivals of the ancient Church were forbidden to those who brought none ; and they were required to be proportioned to the abundance and position of the person offering: "They shall not appear before the LORD empty: every man shall give as he is able, according to the blessing of the LORD thy God, which he hath given thee."* And now, amidst those scenes of glorious and joyful fellowship with God, and testimonies from all the world of the swift and powerful triumphs of his kingdom, and happy and affectionate fellowship of believers, gifts, various gifts, large gifts, loving and expressive gifts, were poured in.

It was not "communism." That is the opposite in its nature. The indiscriminate swinish use of property and its products is to be "common" in its other and evil sense of "unclean." And uncleanness of morals, of family relations, of social habits, and of name, is its necessary result. The charity of the Christians under the inspiration of Pentecost was one which maintained its natural rights. Joses, surnamed Barnabas, was honorably praised for his liberality in selling land, we know not what share of his possessions, and giving the proceeds to the apostles for public uses ; Ananias and Sapphira were smitten of God for falsely pretending to

---

* Deut. xvi. 16, 17.

give what was their "own," and "after it was sold" was in their own power."* The Christians fulfilled the Saviour's command, "Thou shalt love thy neighbor as thyself." This love made them count as common the things which could make each other more useful or more happy, just in the same sense as do among each other the brothers and sisters of an affectionate, pure and true-hearted family. This is the spirit of the New Testament in all its parts.

The first and most profound thought of the gifts which the Christian brought to the house of God was that it was an offering to Christ, his most glorious King. "Because of thy temple at Jerusalem," thy manifestation to men, "shall kings bring presents unto thee." "The kings of Tarshish and the isles shall bring presents. The kings of Sheba and Seba shall offer gifts." "Princes shall come out of Egypt; Ethiopia shall stretch out her hands unto God. Rebuke thou the company of spearmen, till every one submit himself with gifts." Many of these offerings were "*devotional;*" a word which, like others of which we have before spoken, has been degraded into the sense of mere beggarly supplication. It means properly what the psalm says of the thankful tribute which we owe for benefits and deliverances: "Vow, and pay unto the Lord your God; let all that be round about him bring presents unto him that ought to be feared."†

IDEAS OF COMMENTATORS.

This association of reverence and duty is the one which

---

* Acts v. 1-11.

† Ps. lxxvi. 11 and Psalms lxviii. and lxxii.

requires special consideration in the passage in the epistle which contains the inspired Rule for Christian Giving. The first day of the week was the grand memorial, and constant remembrancer, and sure pledge, of all that was most precious to the Christian. Chrysostom, in addressing his people, traced thus the mutual relations of the privileges and duties which are indicated in this text :*

"Mark how he exhorts them in regard to the time ; for truly the day itself was sufficient to lead them to almsgiving. 'Wherefore call to mind,' he says, 'to what ye attained upon this day. All unspeakable blessings, and that event which is the root and beginning of our life, are connected with the day.' Further, the occasion is suitable for the exercise of zealous benevolence, inasmuch as it gives rest and relief from toil, and the spirit thus set free is more disposed to show mercy. And then the partaking of the communion, with its vast and eternal mysteries, itself inspires a spirit of great zeal."

The same observation has been made by numerous modern commentators. One of them says: † "The day itself

---

* *Homily* xliii.

† BURKITT: *Expository Notes on the New Testament.* WORDS-WORTH, also, thus comments upon the connection of the passage: "Observe the beauty of the connection with what was gone before. The Apostle had just been preaching consolation to the faithful, from the certainty of a glorious resurrection of the body; and in accordance with our Lord's declarations concerning works of mercy (Matt. xxv. 34–46) he had taken occasion from that doctrine to enforce the duty of laboring steadfastly in the Lord in deeds of piety and charity, in order to a blessed immortality. He now applies that Christian doctrine and duty to a particular work, in which he him-

doth contain a special motive in it to excite and enlarge our charity; it being the day on which we were begotten to a lively hope, through the resurrection of Jesus Christ from the dead, of an inheritance that is incorruptible. We having therefore received spiritual things from Christ, ought to be more ready to impart our temporal things to Christians."

OBJECTS OF APPROPRIATION OF GIFTS.

How these gifts were appropriated is easily seen in the New Testament and in the history of the early Christians. The all important object was the spread of the gospel. The preachers and teachers who devoted their life and strength to publishing everywhere the knowledge of Christ were provided for, by the apostolic command. " Let him that is taught in the word *communicate* (*bestow a share of the communion* and common gifts) unto him that teacheth, in all good things." The converts from heathenism were so instructed: " For if the Gentiles have been *made partakers* (*communicants*) of their spiritual things, their duty is also to minister unto them in carnal things." *

The poor saints received from the abundant offerings of all, "as every man had need." The profuse, unselfish, heartfelt charity of the Christians was a subject of amazement to the rest of mankind. It was one of the means by which men were convinced of the heavenly character of their faith. The illustrations of it we read with the greatest admiration. They provided for the aged, the widows, the

self was then engaged, and in which he desired to engage the Corinthians."

* Gal. vi. 6. Rom. xv. 27.

sick, lepers, strangers from distant places, support for prisoners, the liberation of slaves, captives, the wants of persons
shipwrecked, the burial of the dead—in which they lovingly
added expensive and odorous spices and ointments—marriage
gifts for poor young women, the transcribing of the books
of Scripture, schools of various kinds for the instruction of
the young, and means for the support of evangelists in cities
and villages, and to foreign and distant nations of the world.
The narratives of the charity of individuals can only be, ex-
plained by the ardent love which they bore to Christ, and
their willingness " to spend and be spent" for him.*

DUTY OF PASTORS NOW; NEED OF THE HOLY SPIRIT.

Such charity can be enkindled now only by basing the
appeals for it upon these grand motives which belong to
" the first day of the week," as the monument of the relations of men to God as their Creator and the God of nature
and providence, to Christ as their Redeemer and their
future Judge, and to the Holy Spirit, the source of all light,
holiness, strength, comfort and joy.   Every Sabbath discourse of the ministry should show to men something of
their obligations in virtue of these great relations.   The first
particular inference which the apostle Paul makes from the
doctrine of the resurrection of the dead is this rule concerning the duty of Christians to lay by of the proceeds of their
labor " as God hath prospered " them.   This most import-

* We are amazed to hear the statement of Chrysostom that the
church at Antioch supported three thousand widows and poor persons.   Many of the widows no doubt were deaconesses, and laborers
in doing good there and elsewhere.

ant duty should be presented constantly "on the first day of the week," as one of the chief themes of the pulpit, and means for the spread of the blessings of the gospel.

What does a pastor or teacher need, in addition to the clear and faithful instruction of a people in the bible principles and motives of giving, in order to succeed in making them liberal? Just one thing. The power of the Holy Ghost in their hearts! Without that, "old Adam is too strong for young Melancthon," and the dominion of mammon over them will remain unbroken. Paul classes liberality as a "grace."* As such it is "the gift of God, through our Lord Jesus Christ." It is bestowed in answer to fervent prayer, in his name. It is one of the streams which the vernal influences of a revival set flowing clear and refreshing, from hearts which had else been all bound up in ice.

* 2 Cor. viii. 9-16.

CHAPTER V.

THE CHURCH THE SUFFICIENT AND RESPONSIBLE AGENCY.

THE starting point of all questions which relate to effective practical charity must be the conviction of the terrible and universal facts

"Of man's first disobedience, and the fruit
Of that forbidden tree, whose mortal taste
Brought death into the world, and all our woe."
"Earth felt the wound, and Nature from her seat
Sighing through all her works, gave signs of woe
That all was lost."
                    "Many shapes
Hath Death, and many are the ways that lead
To his grim cave, all dismal."
                        "Some by violent stroke shall die;
By fire, flood, famine, by intemperance more
In meats and drinks, which on the earth shall bring
Diseases dire."*

The next consideration is: By what combination or agency can those who endeavor to reinstate righteousness, obedience, peace, mercy and temperance, and to restore the ruins of the fall, hope most surely and soon to accomplish their end?

Paradise Lost.

152

The reply is: Through the Church of the Lord Jesus Christ.   For the following reasons.

THE SPECIFIC OBJECT OF THE CHURCH IS REMEDIAL.

First, this is the grand and specific object for which God sent the Son into the world.   It was to bruise the serpent's head, heal those whom he had poisoned, and restore to us security from his power.   When the Son of Jesse shall give a "glorious rest" to our sin-smitten world, "the sucking child shall play on the hole of the asp, and the weaned child shall put his hand on the cockatrice's den."   When Jesus "had called unto him his twelve disciples, he gave them power against unclean spirits, to cast them out, and to heal all manner of sickness and all manner of disease." "He commanded them saying, preach."   But "the sign" of "the kingdom of heaven" was in the associated duty, "heal the sick, cleanse the lepers, raise the dead, cast out devils."*   The Church is the only appointed Divine agency for relieving every kind of human woe.   That is its one special end and business.   It is for healing, and cleansing, and raising up the race trampled and crushed down by Hell.

The Church sins against her Divine Head, she forsakes her Divine mission, when she delegates to the State, and when she resigns to voluntary associations and societies outside of herself, the great and universal trust of applying the means which God gives her to the relief of all the suffering of our race.

Christianity is bound mainly to provide even for the poor

---

* Gen. iii. 15.   Isa. xi. 1.   Matt. x. 1.

of a Christian land. Judaism did so, and does do so, for its poor. Buddhism does so, and is a charitable religion beyond all that the people of this land suppose. Romanism in a large measure does so. Even where poverty abounds, and vice reigns, Protestantism may do so. It was the opinion, very decided, formed from long and most earnest and practical devotion to the subject, to which Dr. Chalmers came, amidst the dark and reeking strongholds of want, vice and wretchedness in the old cities of Glasgow and Edinburgh, that it was the office of Christianity to cure all those ills. His labors as a Christian political economist were directed to the bringing into action of four distinct principles: first, the development of more effective exertion and of greater prudence on the part of the subjects; second, that of mutual charity and beneficence among relations and kindred; third, the extension of a similar spirit among persons who were not kindred; and, after these three means had lifted about three fourths of the burthen, he appealed successfully to the voluntary liberality of the abler classes, who could, and did, easily complete the work. He testified "although I have for many years left the parish, the same system is pursued, and pauperism no longer afflicts this part of the population of Glasgow." He recommended to an English parliamentary committee " the self-extermination of poor rates, simply by a cessation from taking on any new cases."* The soundness, the Christian spirit, and the obligation to try to give effect to, such views as these must deeply impress the soul of one who will

* *Life,* various *Writings;* and *"Reminiscences"* of him and others by JOHN JOSEPH GURNEY.

familiarize himself with the wretchedness, and too often the filth, the indecencies, and the cruel abuses of "charitable institutions" which are supported by the State. "The poor ye have always with you," by a providential arrangement which God constitutes for the moral discipline of man, and from which he exempts the brutes, the birds and the fishes. It certainly was the purpose of the Lord Jesus Christ that his Church should not alone *preach* glad tidings to the poor, but *give* gladness to the poor, in the real relief of their wants and pains. This the Church in America can do through the far greater average wealth of her membership, and the much smaller outlays required in a new world, where pauperism has not taken deep and wide root, or borne its ever-multiplying seed and noxious fruits.

The Congregational Organization.

A *second* great reason why the Church of Christ is the sufficient and responsible agency for the relief and restoration of mankind is, that God has given to each congregation the complete organization which is requisite for that end.

The organization of the individual congregation, as we have it pictured in the New Testament, was thoroughly of a missionary character. The office of the pastor was that of "a shepherd," who goes in and out with his flock, gently leads them—"and they know his voice;" "goes after that which is lost," supports and restores the lame and them that are out of the way; and carries the lambs in his bosom. The elder's office was in many respects, which have been strangely lost sight of in later ages, parallel with that of the pastor. As we have departed far from the aggressive and evangelistic spirit of the New Testament, so we have from the letter.   Let us look at this under another head.

OFFICE OF DEACON.

As we have become careless in giving the temporal blessings of Christ's gospel to the poor, so we have permitted the office which was established with special reference to this duty to entirely lapse in multitudes of our congregations.   We read, in the most definite form, the constitution and duties of the deaconry, amidst the very throbs of Pentecost; and see all of them bearing names which show that they were of foreign birth;* thus indicating the class for whose interests the primitive Church felt the most concern.   The deacons of foreign synagogues seem sometimes to have been charged with the conveyance of money for charitable purposes from one place to another; and similar duties of a benevolent or missionary nature seem to be referred to by Paul when he offers to forward their contributions to the poor, or the sufferers by famine at Jerusalem, through men whom they would "approve by letters," and when again in the second epistle he speaks of one who was "chosen to travel with" him in the performance of the same service.   The office was one transmitted from the synagogue of the Jews, and a prominent feature of its charitable spirit.   The apostle Paul gave to Timothy and Titus special instructions in respect to it.   It is often referred to in the epistles of the early fathers, and the first histories of

* "For the Jews of Palestine were not accustomed to adopt names for their children from the Greek, but from the Hebrew or Syriac languages." MOSHEIM; *Com. on Christians before Constantine*, 153.

the Church. John Calvin traces out Paul's references to the different employments of the deacons. He says:*

"The epistle to the Romans mentions two functions of this kind. 'He that giveth,' says the apostle, 'let him do it with simplicity: he that showeth mercy, with cheerfulness.'† Now, as it is certain that he there speaks of the public officers of the Church, it follows that there were two distinct orders of deacons. Unless my judgment deceive me, the former clause refers to the deacons who administered the alms; and the other to those who devoted themselves to the care of poor and sick persons; such as the 'widows' mentioned by Paul to Timothy.‡ For women could execute no other public office, than by devoting themselves to the service of the poor. If we admit this—and it ought to be fully admitted—there will be two classes of deacons, of whom one will serve the Church in dispensing the property given to the poor, the other in taking care of the poor themselves." It was the distinction of Calvin, and of Calvinism, that—unlike Lutheranism which sought chiefly to purify the existing Church, with no more disturbance than was necessary—he constantly went back to the New Testament to seek its instructions and examples. And thus he adds, quoting Acts vi. 1–3: "See what were the characters of the deacons in the apostolic Church, and what ought to be the characters of ours, in conformity to the primitive example." John Knox and others carefully defined the office in the Scotch Reformation, in the Books of Discipline and others relating to church order. Our pres-

* *Institutes;* b. IV., c. III., ? 9.   † Rom. xii. 8.
‡ 1 Tim. v. 9, 10.

ent Form of Government says, "The Scriptures clearly
point out deacons as distinct officers of the Church, whose
business it is to take care of the poor, and to distribute
among them the collections which may be raised for their
use. To them also may be properly committed the man-
agement of the temporal affairs of the Church."*

OFFICE OF DEACONESSES.

The same spirit of earnest and generous beneficence led
the early Church to appoint an order of deaconesses, such
as Phœbe, "a servant (or *deaconess*) of the Church," the
honored bearer from Corinth of the epistle to the Romans,
of whom Paul said that she had been "a succorer of many,
and of myself also." They were generally widows, made
wise, assiduous and tender in their ministry by their own
afflictions. Such were those whose office and character the
apostle describes in his epistles to Timothy and Titus. Our
pious Presbyterian commentator, Matthew Henry, remarks:
"There was in those times an office in the Church in which
widows were employed; and that was to tend the sick, the
aged, and to look to them by the direction of the deacons."
The writings of the early Christians abound with allusions
to the merciful deeds of deaconesses. Neander says in respect to them, "Although women, in conformity with their
natural destination, were excluded from the offices of
teaching and governing the churches, yet in this manner
the peculiar qualities of females were brought into demand,
as peculiar gifts for the service of the Church." † They are
to be carefully distinguished from the "virgins" who took

* Chap. VI. † *Hist. of Church in First Three Cent's ;* II., I., 1.

upon them in subsequent times vows of celibacy and introduced the practices of Romanism. Calvin presses earnestly,
iu discussing the subject, the distinction between them and
Romanist nuns.* The English Puritans, in like manner,
went back to the New Testament, and "the godly discipline
in the primitive Church;" and about 1576, in an assembly at
Cambridge, adopted certain "conclusions" as to worship;
one of which says : "Touching deacons of both sorts, viz.,
men and women, the Church shall be admonished what is
required by the apostle," etc.† The sphere of woman in

* *Institutes;* IV., xiii., ? xix. "For widows were appointed deaconesses, not to charm God by their songs or unintelligible mutter-
ings, and then spend the rest of their time in idleness; but to serve
the poor on behalf of the whole Church, and to employ themselves
with all attention, earnestness and diligence, in the duties of charity.
Not with a view of performing any service to God in abstaining from
marriage; but only that they might be more at liberty for the discharge of their office. Not in their youth, nor in the flower of their
age, to learn afterward, by late experience, over what a precipice
they had thrown themselves; but, when they appeared to have
passed all danger, they made a vow which was equally consistent
with safety and with piety."

† DAN. NEAL; *Hist. of the Puritans;* I., chap. VI. It is curious
to notice how the lines of a temporary iufluence have, in the case of
JOHN KNOX, given a cast to the subsequent character of an entire
Church. The bitterness of his warfare with Queen Mary prejudiced
him against the office of deaconess. He says, in *"The First Blast
of the Trumpet against the Monstrous Regimen* [or *Government*] *of
Women,"* "Nature doth paint them forth to be weak, frail, unpatient,
feeble and foolish; and experience hath shown them to be uncon-
stant, variable, cruel, and lacking the spirit of counsel and regi-

the Church is enlisting great interest at this time in the European churches. We are beginning to avail ourselves of her peculiar gifts and power for the advancement of various kinds of important work of a missionary kind, both at home and abroad. We saw it in a time of war; why should it not be made still, and far more largely and in varied ways, effective for the peaceful conquests of Christ?

THE OFFICE OF EVANGELIST.

When the Church shall again rouse herself to the task of the conversion of "the whole world" to Jesus Christ, the office of the evangelist will resume its ancient and regular place among her ministry. It is recognized in our Form of Government as one the duties of which are " to preach the gospel, administer sealing ordinances, and organize churches in frontier or destitute settlements."* By consulting the epistles to Timothy and Titus, who filled this office, it will be seen that it is an office widely different from that of the pastor. The experiences of the home, but especially of the foreign, missionary in this age prove that such is the case. It is one of itinerancy, of superintendence, of preparation of the way for more settled "incumbents" of the ministerial functions. The nature of the office, and its im-

men." *Hist. of Reformation* and other *Writings:* p. 443. Knox's countryman, Sir WALTER SCOTT, in *Marmion*, wrote more wisely:

> "O woman! in our hours of ease,
> Uncertain, coy and hard to please,
> When pain and anguish wring the brow,
> A ministering angel thou l"

* Chap. XVI. § xv.

portance to the Church of Christ, in her higher and "evan-gelistic" aims, are well set forth in an article which appeared recently from the pen of an esteemed missionary in India, to which we are glad to be able to refer.*

It is plain that just as God appointed completely all the departments of the former Levitical service, which was in many respects a type of the designs of the Church of Christ, so he did not leave to chance the arrangements of that Church itself; which are most vital as earthly means to the sufficient maintenance of its ministry, the education of those called to the sacred office, the costs of its worship, and the promulgation of its doctrines and the communication of its blessings to every creature. The efficiency of this or-ganization is illustrated in the wonderful history of the first centuries, which records the triumph of the Christian relig-ion over the superstition and opposition of men, its spread over the civilized world, and its establishment amidst many dark and barbarous nations.

WHY HAVE THESE OFFICES LAPSED?

It is then a most important question for us to ask, Why have these scriptural offices of the deacon and deaconess fallen into disuse in the Presbyterian Church, which in most features so nearly follows the apostolic model? Is it not because it has lost so much of that humane consideration for the classes to which those offices ministered? It is a startling and unwelcome suggestion to make against our

* *Presbyterian Quarterly and Princeton Review:* April, 1874. Art. VII. By Rev. S. H. Kellogg, of Allahabad.

11

own honored and dear "household of faith." But what
thoughtful Presbyterian minister. or church member, has
not been smitten in conscience by the unconcerned way in
which we have sometimes handed over the sick to the hospitals of the State, or left them to be cared for in those of
Romanist or other churches; given over the Christian poor
to the desolateness, the icy and graceless provisions, and
the vicious associations of the common almshouse; and
left sometimes, alas! even the disabled and crippled and
friendless minister, the brave but invalid soldier of the cross,
who has worn himself out in hard conflicts, toils and trials for
the Church, and has impoverished his family by his unflinch-
ing fidelity to her interests, to "the providence of God;"
or to the consideration of the possible benefits of a life-
insurance company,* whose "policy" he has not money to
buy, and whose system is as foreign and inefficacious in *his*
case as the thought of it is discreditable to the fellowship
of the Church of our blessed and merciful Saviour.

The conclusion which presses upon us as Christians in this
age is, that side by side with our earnest and vigorous efforts to
rouse the membership of the Church to a return to the New
Testament standard of consecration in the matters of money
and property to the service of Christ, stands the obligation
to completely organize the Church itself in conformity with
that order which the great Captain of our salvation appointed when it started forth, in the flush of its first zeal and
courage, to the conquest of the whole world.

* This is not intended to be an objection to ordinary investments
by those who have the means, in these business associations, if safe
and well conducted. In this light they are very useful,

SUPERINTENDENCE OF WORK BY CHURCH COURTS.

A *third* reason why the Church should be the great agency of religious beneficence is, that God has ordained a succession of courts for the "mutual counsel and assistance necessary in establishing his kingdom, to preserve soundness of doctrine and regularity of discipline, and to enter into common measures for promoting knowledge and religion, and for preventing infidelity, error, and immorality."[*] These great designs cannot be combined and managed by any other instrumentality of men, by any civil power, or by any voluntary associations of Christians.

The Church is a queen whose government and offices are administered in the behalf of Jesus Christ, whose bride she is, and with the pledge of the co-operation of the Holy Ghost, who hath made her servants "overseers" of the work of Christ. She is a "body" vitally connected with a divine Head, and "the fullness of him that filleth all in all." "We are members of his body, of his flesh, and of his bones."[†]

It is then the office of the Church, by its successive representative courts, to arrange the various departments of operation which are necessary for the spread of the gospel and extension of Christ's kingdom over the world, to superintend their work, and to take, as our book says, all necessary "measures for promoting knowledge," through the inculcation of principles and the communication of information; "and religion," through the maintenance of the means by

---

[*] Form of Government, chap. x., § 1.

[†] Acts xx. 28. Eph. i. 23; v. 30.

which it is made effective unto the salvation of men. It is the Church's place to baptize and religiously instruct the youth, to select and to educate those who are adapted and called of God to the ministry; to maintain the settled ministry and ordinances of religion; to send forth evangelists to the destitute in this land, and to the unenlightened and perishing in all pagan and anti-christian lands; to arm these men and women with all the apparatus of evangelical literature and publications which the age affords; to support them with all other auxiliary means of reaching, and saving, and lifting up to a position as blest as our own, all those for whom Christ shed his precious blood; and to be a heavenly organization to do just what the Lord Jesus if he were presiding in his incarnate form over his kingdom here would say to his servants to do, in order that every soul on earth may be drawn to do his will "*as it is done in heaven.*" In all this glorious round of employments each court of the Church has its responsible place, from the greatest to the least, that the whole may be thoroughly vitalized, energized, and made efficient for the divine ends. It is a grand celestial work, in which an angel feels honored to say, "I am thy fellow-servant," and which the heavenly principalities "look into" with joy and delight to the praise of their and our King!*

To the accomplishment of this heavenly mission the most necessary material instrumentality is "the gold and the silver" which God created for the great end of advancing the glory of his kingdom. He gives the "prosperity" by which "every one" of his sons and daughters obtains or accumulates any share of it and the property which it represents. And the Church can only prosper in her earthly

* 1 Pet. i. 12. Rev. xix. 10.

charge when each one of her membership contributes and performs his part in the spirit of that Divine Rule which we are considering. If the Church is beaten back, and defeated in any field of attack, it is chiefly because one or another soldier or company has faltered and disobeyed orders. The failure of a few in some one place has disheartened many others. And thus perhaps a great effort is thwarted, the world and Satan rejoice, and our King is humiliated and displeased.

CHAPTER VI.

PRIMARY SECULAR OBJECT OF SABBATH GIVING, PERIODICITY.

WE turn from the religious aspects of the appointment to give " on the first day of the week" to those which are secular. Here also we may discern the hand of infinite wisdom in making it.

A few years ago the writer had a conversation with a well-known financier, whose abilities and experience were of eminent service in developing the national resources during the late rebellion, in regard to the means by which those of the Christian Church are to be brought out, in order to meet the requirements of her great war with sin. " *The first thing* to be secured," said he, emphatically, "is *periodicity.*" This weighty remark would be reaffirmed by every financier and political economist, and business man and lawyer.

THE FOUNDATION STONE OF FINANCIAL OPERATIONS.

"Periodicity" is the foundation stone of extensive financial operations. Whatever the term of the recurring period may be—let it be annual, or semi-annual, or quarterly, or monthly, or weekly, or by any other equal divisions of time —yet this is the necessary condition of all honest and secure pecuniary business, that its payments be faithfully made at definite times.

166

This fundamental law is so vital to business transactions that failure punctually to fulfill its obligations at once depreciates the value of the stock of any railroad, or bank, or factory, or community.   Reliability as to regular payments enhances the credit of such paper, in proportion to the ground of it.   The rate of interest required is increased or decreased in proportion as it is the pledge of a community or a nation, of an uncertain or a stable government, upon which men have to depend for the periodical returns upon their investments.   Business men anxiously arrange to meet the recurring payments which rents, and salaries, and obligations for the materials of trade and manufactures, necessarily impose upon them.   And every corporation, commercial or political, lays its plans to provide for the fulfillment of its regular obligations.

The business obligations of congregations, and also those of the organizations appointed by the Church at large which are dependent upon the contributions of the congregations, are in like manner periodic.   Annual payments, quarterly or monthly payments, and other obligations which are regular as to time, are, and must be, incurred by them; the violations of which are certainly as culpable and injurious to their public credit and respect as similar failures of the people and institutions of the world are in their case.   Those of Christians are indeed more objectionable; for however the charity and patience of religious people may excuse them and submit to them, they are the fruitful themes of scoffers, the scorn of the honorable men of this world, the stumbling-block of the doubting and perplexed, and the shame of the conscientious and faithful.   They compel the minister, the student for the ministry, the missionary, and every one who has made engagements upon the faith of them, to be guilty of untruth and injustice. They hinder the extension and success of the gospel of Christ. Thus they are the ruin of immortal souls. They are fresh wounds to the Saviour.

A public financier sees and strikes at the root of the difficulty when he says, The Church's expenses, like the State's, are periodic: her income should be regulated as to the method of supply, and that be also periodic. Otherwise failures, disasters, dishonor, depreciation, are inevitable. The contributions of church members ought to be made "regular," that is, *according to a rule*. Those of Boards and of congregations, which are the clock's face, on which the world looks and which exhibits the results, can only be trustworthy when each wheel and each pinion and each piece of every kind moves in harmony with the end in view; all different but all punctual.

VAST INFLUENCE OF THIS LAW.

The influence of this law extends over all the employments of man. It affects usefulness, comfort, health, life, and all the great ends of life, in ways which are countless; in ways which become more important to our eyes in proportion to our comprehension of them and of the great designs of the Divine education of man on earth.

Until three centuries ago the world had no means of securing perfect periodicity in instruments for measuring time. The clumsy clepsydra, or water-clock, the sand-glass, the sun-dial, were those which were most accurate. An Italian

youth, born in the same year with Calvin's death, a student
at Pisa, who was disgusted with the rubbish of monastic instruction, stood one day watching the regular vibrations of a
heavy bronze lamp which hung, and does so yet, from the
centre of the dome of the cathedral. He had discovered
in them the great problem of regulating time! No subsequent one of the many debts of the world to Galileo was so
valuable as this. The pendulum and the balance-wheel
have now been perfected, so that the astronomer accurately
distinguishes and registers time by the thousandth parts of
one second. Innumerable important acquisitions in science,
and in the arts, have been imparted to us through this gift.
We can measure now the laws of light, and sound, and motion, of the subtle and the mighty forces of nature, and of
the movements and influences of the heavenly bodies. We
mark the boundaries of land. We navigate safely the ocean.
We can fix exactly, by the comparison of the moment of
noon with that of the chronometer on board which retains
the time of Greenwich, the spot where our ship rolls, in
the Atlantic, or Indian, or Pacific ocean, in the tropical or
in the arctic seas; and thus know also her speed, her
course, and many of her possible dangers.

Just as glorious, we may conceive, to the Almighty God
as the work of creating the countless globes of matter, is the
omnipotent propulsion and control of each one in its course;
so that it returns, unless retarded by other bodies, to the
same spot in its orbit, after a career of hundreds or thousands of millions of miles, at the appointed instant, century
after century, without a variation of one minute of time.
This infinitely perfect government of nature is the highest

and most impressive illustration of his perfect moral government. Its "line is gone through all the earth;" its "words to the end of the world." It says to every heart of man: "The judgments of the LORD are true and righteous altogether." "The statutes of the Lord are right, rejoicing the heart." "The testimony of the Lord is sure, making wise the simple." *

The Scriptures of the Old Testament were not understood until, to close the Old Dispensation, the Spirit of God was poured upon the eyes of mankind; then they saw their perfection, and cried, "we know that the law is spiritual, but I am carnal, sold under sin; who shall deliver me from the body of this death? I thank God; through Jesus Christ our Lord." And, in turn, Nature has not been understood till these "latter days" of the New Dispensation; but is now revealed to us by the goodness and grace of Him who has furnished us with means to explore, and discover, and bring forth its wondrous mysteries. We find infinite attributes of God; infinite grace in Christ who justified us from the guilt of sin; infinite relationships of man; infinite perfection of duty; infinite prospects of heavenly education and service, and recompenses of joys, and hopes of glory; illustrated to us, in the knowledge which he is revealing through the works of his hands.

To impress upon the Church of God, in ways suited to the Hebrew race, to their agricultural and pastoral life, and to the typical and preparatory character of all their religious institutions, these grand, primary, fundamental ideas, was one of the chief objects of the appointments of the Levitical

* Ps. xix.

dispensation.   This for two great reasons : first, that through the revelations to the Jews all men may know *sin*, and thus be driven to the only atonement for it, the blood of the incarnate Son of God ; second, that they may measure *duty*—"Be ye perfect, even as your Father which is in heaven is perfect."   The returns of the moon, of the first ripening of the grain, of the harvest home, of the maturing of successive generations of animals ; the sabbatic impress upon weeks, and months, and years and weeks of years ; the marking of the eras of infancy and adolescence ; and many such appointments for religious duties and offerings, were a ceaseless and powerful education of the ancient people in the one principle of the consecration of *time*, in all its revolutions, to the Great Creator and Lord of all.

The Christian is called to "spiritualize" these principles ; to be fully devoted to God, not for law, but out of love to Jesus ; not with the thought of merit, but in the cultivation of grace upon grace ; not to the exaltation of self, but to the glory of God, only and for ever and ever.

CHAPTER VII.

SABBATH GIVING REQUIRES FREQUENCY.

ALONG with the principle of periodicity Sabbath giving establishes its most important qualification, that is, frequency.

NECESSARY TO THE OBJECTS OF A MISSIONARY CHURCH.

To comprehend this appointment we must plant ourselves in the position of the first Christians. Over the cross of the dying Redeemer was nailed the inscription which declared him to be the Messianic KING. When he ascended, he commanded his disciples, "Preach the gospel to every creature." The first preachers cried, "The promise is to you, and to your children, and to all that are afar off." The first written expositions of doctrine said, "The Scriptures foreseeing that God would justify the heathen through faith, preached the gospel unto Abraham, saying, In thee shall all nations be blessed."* A burning, restless, all-sacrificing zeal for the preaching of the glad tidings of salvation through Jesus to all the world, inflamed their whole nature. They were a sincere missionary body.

Frequent giving was a necessity to such men and such women. They could not help, lovingly, in faith, joyfully, bestowing all the means that they could command, when-

* Gal. iii. 8. Acts ii. 39. Mark xvi. 15.

172

ever the opportunity for its suitable use occurred. As this opportunity was offered every Sabbath, gifts were a regular part of the worship of the day and its accompaniment.

It does not appear that every church member contributed on every Sabbath. As will be shown in a future chapter, this was not the divine rule which the apostle gave. Every one was taught to "lay by in store as God had prospered," and from this stock to bring as he considered the occasion to require. And yet every Sabbath afforded opportunities of some kind or other, and was honored with gifts from many of the worshipers.

The rekindling of missionary zeal, by any extraordinary circumstances of the Church, such as a great revival of religion, or a general chastisement of sorrow or of loss, tends ever to inspire a return to this scriptural and primitive frequency of gifts.

Such, for example, were the circumstances of the Scotch Free Church when, in 1842, in contending for the right to choose its own spiritual teachers, it suddenly found itself deprived of the pecuniary supports of the government, upon which it had existed. As a Church, by one vote of its General Assembly its ministry elected poverty, hunger, nakedness, for Christ. And they were more than conquerors through him who loved them.

The plan which was adopted under the intelligent and able leadership of Dr. Chalmers, to organize a financial system to meet the immediate and vast necessities for church buildings, manses, salaries, schools, colleges, the poor, church extension at home, the Jewish and other foreign missions, was based on " weekly contributions, from the penny or twopence a week to the larger contributions of those who are both willing and wealthy." To gather these sums there were appointed an elder and deacon for each district in a congregation, to superintend the work. "The deacon might, or might not, be a collector himself," but should "at least once a quarter accompany each of the collectors who operate within his sphere, throughout all the families, and by means of conversation, as well as by the distribution of tracts and periodicals, sustain their interest in the cause." The collectors were expected "to give half an hour a week, if needed, or two hours a month, to the service." The result was a grand, blessed, honorable and permanent success; and it proved that "the tendency is to elevate the platform of humble life; and the effect of its payments, so far from being to impoverish or depress, is, through the medium of character and principle, or by the elastic operation of moral causes, to raise and uphold our people in a far higher economic status."*

EDUCATIONAL INFLUENCE OF FREQUENT GIVING.

The effect of frequent giving is a most important one to the experience of the individual believer. We live in an age and a land of "fulness of bread," which, as of old, causes people to forget to "strengthen the hand of the poor and the needy."

It was one of the most pointed and emphatic warnings of God when he brought Israel into the promised land, "Beware lest, when thou hast eaten and art full, and hast

* *Economics of the Free Church of Scotland,* Sec. i., Arts. 3 and 6.

built goodly houses and dwelt therein, and thy flocks and thy herds multiply, and thy gold and thy silver is multiplied, and all that thou hast is multiplied, then thine heart be lifted up and thou forget the LORD thy God." The divine warnings proved but too well founded. Great and repeated kindnesses, if unreciprocated or unacknowledged, ordinarily excite, first gratitude, then self-complacency, then indifference, and when the consciousness of obligation becomes at length oppressive and painful, aversion and hostility.

Frequent regular giving is a remembrancer to men's own hearts, and an acknowledgment to God, of some momentous facts. First, it keeps before men's minds the multitude of God's tender mercies; "I will come into thy house in the multitude of thy mercy." Then that their regularity, so far from hardening the heart and shutting out the sense of personal care and favor under the impression of its being a "law" or "order of nature," is a motive for higher thankfulness and love; "blessed be the LORD who daily loadeth us with benefits, even the God of our salvation." And thus men are humbled for sin against him whose "goodness leadeth us to repentance," and led to preparation for "the day of wrath and revelation of the righteous judgment of God, who will render to every man according to his deeds."*

There was a tendency, immediately upon the acceptance of the doctrine of free grace by those whom it relieved from legal bondage, and who but partly comprehended the nature of the "law of the spirit of life in Christ Jesus," to neglect

---

* Ps. v. 7; lxviii. 19. Rom. ii. 4, 5.

Christian practical duties. The epistles of the New Testament abound with the admonition that it was a more spiritual "law," a "perfect law of liberty."*

The most ancient, spiritual, and beautiful Christian tract outside of the books of the New Testament is the first epistle of Clement, of whom Paul so tenderly wrote from Rome as a "fellow-laborer" "whose name is in the book of life."† It was written to these same Corinthians to whom Paul addressed the Divine Rule for Giving. Clement reminds them that we should "take care that we perform our offerings and services to God at their appointed seasons, for these he has commanded to be done, not by chance and disorderly, but at certain determinate times and hours. Therefore he has ordained, by his supreme will and authority, both where and through what persons they are to be performed, that so, all things being piously done unto all well pleasing, they may be acceptable to him. They therefore who make their offerings at the appointed seasons are happy and accepted."‡

CHRISTIANITY IS TO BE ADAPTED TO THE POOR.

It is one of the deepest principles of Christianity that it is, and must be, adapted *to the poor.* After Jesus Christ was inaugurated to his priesthood by the baptism of John, and appeared for the first time in the village of his youth to preach, the text of his sermon, from the prophecies of Isaiah, began with these words, "The Spirit of the Lord is upon me, because he hath anointed me to preach the gospel

---

* Rom. viii. 2.   Jas. i. 25.   † Phil. iv. 3.   ‡ *First Epistle to Corinthians,* sec. xl.

to the poor." It is a religion which digs at the base of the mountain until it shall fall.

The institutions of Christianity must ever be adapted to the wants, and employments, and interests of the poor. Chrysostom, explaining our Rule to his church at Antioch, exhorts them to conform to the words of the apostle, for, says he, "by his not enjoining them to deposit all at once, he makes his counsel easy, since the gathering by little and little hinders all perception of the burthen and the cost." This method is a constant incitement to economy, and hence to industry, honesty, and temperance. It creates warm and practical sympathies for the suffering, by the weekly consideration of their claims, and of the measure of relief that is needed for them. And the actual provision for the poor by the Church can best be effected when there is a weekly and appropriate supply of funds, or of such materials and articles as are required for the cases which are continually brought before it, varied by the wants and calamities of common life. A Christianity which is to run in a continuous, pure, and refreshing stream of supply requires ever-flowing sources.

Secular Ideas of Frequent Giving.

To make the wisdom of this feature of the Divine Rule manifest to every mind, let us observe for a moment the practices of men in secular affairs.

It seems a very little thing to pay a quarter of a cent tax upon your daily morning cup of coffee and evening cup of tea. But the income from all the daily cups in the country paid the government ten or twelve millions of dollars a year dur-

12

ing our war.   It is a very minute contribution for you to pay the one hundredth part of one cent tax upon each of the matches with which every day your lamps and fires are lighted; yet one factory of those matches returns to the government a revenue for stamps of three hundred and sixty thousand dollars a year.   Thus we realize how it is, chiefly, that a government is enabled to make the stupendous outlays of hundreds of millions of dollars a year in time of war, simply by means of loans, the interest of which, and in time the principal, is obtained from small assessments upon things which most persons want every day.   Thus also may frequent little sums be made sufficient for the Church's conflicts with the powers of sin.

We may see the same principle made available in numerous forms in the commercial world.   The division of payments is a common device which makes many a difficult enterprise successful.   A railroad pushes stock upon the market in quarterly payments, which would at one payment be taken by but a few persons.   A publisher sells a heavy edition of an expensive illustrated work in monthly parts, which not one purchaser in fifty would obtain if sold entire. A sewing machine company induces hundreds of poor working women to buy its machines, upon agreements to pay by small sums out of their weekly wages, who would not dare to attempt the payment of the same amount at one time.

This is one of the wisest features of the Divine financial plan, which every Christian should learn.   Even some poor laboring men might be induced to bring in the rounds of the year what would amount to an average of fifty cents a Sabbath, "according as God prospered" them.   They would be really surprised to find that fifty-two times fifty cents is twenty-six dollars. One of them could not have spared it, in his judgment previously, amidst his wants for house-rent and children's clothing, and the grocer's demands. But at the close of the year he sees that he has done so, and is none the poorer; and he holds his head up, a happier and stronger Christian and man, with the confidence that he has made a considerable deposit in the bank of providence, and also in the treasury of heaven, for himself and his wife and children. He has made an investment in the eternal promises, which causes trials and troubles to be less dreaded, and makes him hear the word of God with new interest, assurance and profit. This principle of the division of payments for good objects is the secret by which he has accumulated a great wealth of blessings.

CHAPTER VIII.

INDIVIDUAL RESPONSIBILITY.

THE influence of the Holy Spirit in conversion and sanctification is to open the eyes of a man to see the power, and holiness, and majesty of God. His experience is like that of John at Patmos: "When I saw him, I fell at his feet as dead. And he laid his right hand upon me, saying, Fear not, I am the first and the last; I am he that liveth and was dead, and behold I am alive for evermore." Thenceforth he lies at the feet of his glorified Saviour. He walks with him. He talks with him. Jesus is the first and the last in his honor and love. The right hand of his Lord rests upon him. It gives him joy, courage, power, and patience. Oh, how blessed to *feel* that hand of him that liveth for evermore!

The object of the word of God is to make religion personal. It is all addressed to YOU. The commandments each say, " *Thou* shalt not have any other gods before me ;" "*thou* shalt not take the name of the Lord *thy* God in vain ;" and "*thou* shalt not" commit any sin. Jesus says, "when *thou* prayest, enter into thy closet ; pray in secret." "When *thou* fastest, appear not unto men to fast, but unto *thy* Father which is in secret." "When *thou* doest thine alms, let thine alms be in secret, and *thy* Father which seeth

in secret shall reward *thee* openly." Jacob, the great model
of prayer, was "left *alone*" when he obtained the great
blessings of Peniel. Jesus loved to pray "alone;" to ex-
pound his parables to his disciples "alone."

This is the spirit of our divine rule for Christian beneficence, "let *every one*" lay by and contribute. It is a matter of personal responsibility to Jesus Christ. It is a duty
directly related, in this epistle from the pen of Paul, to the
doctrine of the resurrection from the dead; it is an immediate inference from the prospects of that last and great
day.

It is very striking to trace out the most important applications of this same pronoun,* as made by Paul in this epistle. Men are prone to distinguish "positive" from "natural" obligations and duty. The former class require therefore to be made authoritative and pointed. This pronoun,
translated "every one," occurs twenty-three times in this
one epistle which relates principally to the "ordinances"
of the Christian Church, while it is found but twenty-four
times altogether in the thirteen other epistles from his hand.
Several of the passages in which it is found bear most
strongly upon the duty which he states in this crowning
rule. Addressing the members of the Corinthian Church,
and all believers, as it were individually, he says "*every man*
hath his proper gift of God, one after this manner and
another after that;" "now hath God set the members *every
one* of them in the body as it hath pleased him;" "let no
man seek his own, but *every man* another's wealth;" "*every
man's* work shall be made manifest, for the day (of judg-

* ἕκαστος.

ment) shall declare it; because it shall be revealed by fire, and the fire shall try *every man's* work of what sort it is;" then as to the resurrection, "*every man* in his own order, Christ the first-fruits, afterward they that are Christ's at his coming;" and finally, in behalf of the great work of Christian charity, "upon the first day of the week let *every one* of you lay by him in store as God hath prospered him." In these and several kindred passages the Greek pronoun used is the same. The apostle designs to include every person created by God, every one who is redeemed by the blood of his Son, every one enjoying the gifts of divine grace, every one living in the world, every one who is to be raised from the dead; *all* must *give* to the work of Christ. It was the application of the Saviour's own words: "For the Son of man shall come in the glory of his Father, with his holy angels: then shall he reward *every man* according to his works."*

The power of the Holy Spirit in the lives of believers or in revival of the Church has ever wrought this deep sense of personal responsibility to God as to the use of the pecuniary means of serving him with which men are entrusted. Many instances will occur to every reader from the lives of eminent Christians. Take, for example, that of Richard Baxter. He says: "My rule has been to study to need as little as possible for myself; to lay out nothing on need-nots; to live frugally on little; to serve God on what he allowed me, so that what I took for self might be as good work for the common good as that which I gave to others; and then to do all the good I could with the rest. The more

* 1 Cor. vii. 7; xii. 18; x. 24; iii. 12–18; xv. 23; xvi. 2. Matt. xvi. 27.

I have done this, the more I have had to do it with; for the glory of God's grace, he will be no man's debtor. When I gave away almost all, the more came in, I scarce know how, when unexpected and unplanned for. When by improvidence I was led to use too much on myself, or on things of little importance, then I prospered less than when I did otherwise. If I had planned to give only after my death, then all might have been lost; whereas, when I gave away at present, and trusted to God for the future, then I wanted nothing and lost nothing."

With what anxious and pathetic entreaty, like that of the apostle Paul, as if in the very sight of the resurrection and the judgment, does Baxter appeal to those whose hearts are wrapt up in the things of this present world, and who forget the account which they must give to God. His words may well stir us all to more devotedness to God in all that we possess. "Remember how short a time thou must keep and enjoy the wealth which thou hast gotten. How quickly thou must be stripped of all! Canst thou keep it when thou hast it? Canst thou make a covenant with death, that it shall not call away thy soul? Thou knowest beforehand that thou art of short continuance, and the world is but thy inn and passage, and that a narrow grave for thy flesh to rot in is all that thou canst keep of thy largest possessions, save what thou layest up in heaven, by laying it out in obedience to God. How short is life! How quickly gone! Thou art almost dead and gone already! What are a few days or a few years more? And wilt thou make so much ado for so short a life? And so careful a provision for so short a stay? Yea, how uncertain is thy time, as well as short! Thou canst not say what world thou shalt be in to-morrow. Remember, man, that thou must die! Thou must die! Thou must quickly die! Thou knowest not how soon! Breathe yet a few breaths more, and thou art gone! And yet canst thou be covetous and drown thy soul with earthly cares? Dost thou soberly read thy Saviour's warning (Luke xii. 19–21)? Is it not spoken as to thee? 'Thou fool, this night thy soul shall be required of thee; then whose shall those things be which thou hast provided? So is every one that layeth up riches for himself, and is not rich toward God.' . . . Remember, man, that thou hast another world to live in, and a far longer life to make provision for, and that thou must be in heaven or hell for ever. This is true, whether thou believe it or not, and thou hast no time but this to make thy preparation in, and as thou believest, and livest, and laborest now, it must go with thee to all eternity."*

It is this deep sense of individual responsibility to God, in the use of the property and means of doing good which he has put in our hands, which this feature of the Divine Rule is designed to awaken and sustain. May the spirit of Richard Baxter possess our hearts, and his devoted liberality be an example which shall influence our lives.

* *Practical Theology,* chap. iv.

CHAPTER IX.

THE UNIVERSAL PRIVILEGE OF GIVING.

THERE were great rejoicings on those grand occasions when the whole nation of Israel met in Jerusalem, several times in the year, to commemorate God's goodness in the gifts of nature, or in its deliverances from enemies. It was partially joined in by many converts, or sympathizing friends, who were present from other races of people.

But when they went up to the temple, impassable lines of separation were drawn between families and neighbors. The Roman centurion who loved the people and had built them a synagogue, the Greek or Syrian proselyte to the religion of Jehovah, or even the Idumean king, Herod, who rebuilt the temple, was only permitted to enter a great outer court. It was splendidly adorned with columns of polished stone, and surrounded with spacious cloisters and porticoes; but the stranger was confronted with a wall, and an inscription forbidding him further access on pain of death. His gifts must be left in a place polluted with money changers and them that sold doves to the very poor. Within that wall the Jewish family of worshipers passed; but there the wife and the daughter were stopped from going further with their male kindred. It was the place where things devoted and given as oblations were left, and where were the treasuries; but it was that in which those suspected of leprosy or of ceremonial uncleanness were detained, and subjected to the inspection of the priestly physician. It was counted still unholy ground. An ascent and still another low partition wall might be passed by the men; but they in turn were shut from the area upon which stood the glorious temple, in front of which was the great altar of sacrifices. They might pray where they were, and join in the chorus of the Levitical choir; but only the priesthood dared enter that sacred place. And still another barrier was drawn, a thick, dark veil, to cover the holiest of all, within which the high priest entered once a year. To him alone was granted communion with him that dwelt between the cherubim; and approach to the mercy seat, and to the ark in which were the manna, and the rod that budded and the tables of the law.*

Thank God that from those courts one who had authority scourged the money changers, and the covetous and the unclean, and opened them all to be "a house of prayer for all people." "Barbarian, Scythian, bond and free," are one in Christ Jesus. The middle walls of partition are all and for ever broken down, and taken clean away. The veil itself was rent in twain from the top to the bottom when Jesus cried, "It is finished." Now "every one," the women, the strangers, the sick and the lame, the priests and the people alike, may come and offer gifts and plead the perfect sacrifice for sin to one that is able to save them from death.†

* JOSEPHUS; Antiq., XV. xi. 5, 6, 7.   Heb. ix. and x.

† Isa. lv. 7.   Mark xi. 17.   Col. iii. 11.   Eph. iii. 14, 15.   Matt. xxvii. 51.

EVERY CLASS OF WORSHIPERS SHOULD BRING GIFTS.

In this temple the gifts of all are welcome:* In a heathen temple one of the most affecting sights is the crowds of women, who are the chief supporters of religion in every land, however their rights may be denied by the stronger sex. They bring their sacrifices and gifts; and, what is far more important, they bring their children, and teach them to lift up in their little hands the offerings to the gods, and then to fold their hands together and bow down and make their requests of the gods. They often give them to the priesthood, and cherish hopes thence of peculiar favor from heaven upon the family. What lessons this religiousness of those who only enjoy the dim light of nature teaches us who have clearer light, and thence higher duties and accountability!

Children should be taught to bring their glad gifts to Jesus. When on earth he loved them dearly. He took them up in his arms, and blessed them. He told his disciples to imitate them. He was welcomed as king, to Jeru-

* DR. HODGE; *Exposition,* makes the following comment upon this in the rule, "*Let every one of you.* It was an important feature of these apostolic arrangements, that the contributions were not to be confined to any one class of the people. The same amount might perhaps have been raised from the rich few. But this would not have answered one important end which the apostle had in view. It was the religious effect which these gifts were to produce in promoting Christian fellowship, in evincing the truth and power of the gospel, and in calling forth gratitude and praise to God, even more than the relief of the temporal necessities of the poor, that Paul desired to see accomplished. 2 Cor. ix. 12–14."

salem, by their hosannas. Their songs in many tongues are making him king over multitudes of hearts to-day. This is one of the "signs" of his approaching reign on earth. Since the Reformation the Church has taught children doctrine by catechisms; it has taught them praise in music and songs: now it owes to childhood to teach it to bring gifts to the king, which is the highest token of its pure love.

Woman should come with numerous gifts. Christ is the Son of God, and the son of woman, not in truth of man: the son of Mary, not of Joseph. Woman sat lowliest at his feet to hear his word. She called for no sword, and made no boasts; and yet,

"Not she with traitorous kiss her Saviour stung;
Not she blasphemed him with unholy tongue.
She, when apostles shrunk, could danger brave;
Last at the cross and earliest at the grave."

If man is the representative head in religious things, woman is the heart. The Bible is full of the most lovely pictures of the love of God and of Christ to woman, and of woman's loyalty, especially to the person of the Saviour. And it is this *personal* love which gives true devotedness, strength and joy to faith in him. Woman was first to bless his mother when the angel announced the promise of his birth. Women's hands were first to minister to him as a helpless babe; women the first to bring spices which they had prepared, very early in the morning, when it was yet dark, to the sepulchre; and to wonder and be affrighted, to see the two men in shining garments, and to cry with fear

and great joy: "Rabboni, Master," when he left it as conqueror over death and hell. The heaviest curse of sin is
upon woman; and she is correspondingly lifted up by the
gospel. The heathen, when the Church began its course,
exclaimed, "What wives these Christians have!" This
present time is again an era of woman's honor and usefulness. Her gifts are rescuing our missionaries from disheart-
enment, and arming them for enlarged efforts. Now "let
every one of you," says the word of God to them, come
with her best gifts; be they a Samuel, with three bullocks,
and an ephah of flour, and a bottle of wine; or an alabas-
ter box of ointment of spikenard, very precious; or be they
but two mites, the "all" of her penury. Jesus loves *your*
offerings. The treasury of the old temple was in the Court
of the Women. Women have very much to do now, in the
building of the spiritual temple. The work of their hands,
and their costly stones, and their silver and gold, are needed
to make it a glory in all lands.

"Every" poor man should bring gifts. Christ was poor.
The apostles were poor men. The first Christians were
nearly all poor men. "Yet making many rich." Do you
wish to know who were the imperial family of this world,
and how they looked, and what they did, in the days of the
emperor Domitian? Then look at this strange and touching picture, handed down by Eusebius, and take courage, thou
poor man, from it. The historian thus describes their ar-
raignment before the Roman emperor:* "Of the family
of the Lord there were yet living the grandchildren of

* *Eccles. Hist.*, iii.   He quotes from a still earlier writer, Hege-
sippus.

Jude, called the brother of our Lord according to the flesh. These persons were reported to the government as being of the family of David, and were brought to Domitian by the officers appointed to enlist the people; for this emperor was as fearful in regard to the appearance of Christ as Herod was. He put to them the question whether they were of David's race? They confessed that they were. He then asked them what possessions they had, or how much money? Both of them answered, that they possessed between them the value of only about nine thousand silver pence;* and that this they had not in silver, but in a piece of land containing only thirty-nine acres, from which they raised the amount needed for their taxes, and supported themselves, by their own labor. Then they also began to show their hands, and exhibited the firmness of their bodies, and the callous places formed on their hands by incessant toil, as the evidence that they were laboring men. They were then asked further respecting Christ and his kingdom, what was its nature, and when and where it was to appear? They replied, that it was not a temporal nor earthly kingdom, but a celestial and angelic one; that it would appear at the end of the world, and that then, coming in glory, Christ would judge the quick and the dead, and give to every one according to his works. Upon this Domitian, despising them, made no reply, but treating them contemptuously as simpletons he commanded them to be dismissed, and by a decree ordered the persecution to cease. Thus delivered, they ruled the churches, both as witnesses and

* Less than fifteen hundred dollars in our present silver money. Money was worth more then than now; probably land was not so.

relatives of the Lord. When peace was established, they continued living even until the times of Trajan."

And yet these poor, hard-handed, despised, laboring men were "the brothers," or, as we say now, "the cousins," of the personal family of Jesus Christ. His own employment in youth was no doubt that of a carpenter. Yet he came into the world to be of such as these; and they were the men who conquered the world—not with swords and spears; but with the universal preaching of salvation, with works of mercy, with patient suffering, with almsgiving, and with love. Jesus "lifted up his eyes on his disciples and said, Blessed be ye poor, for yours is the kingdom of God."* The poor formed its conquering legions then, and they must do so now.†

And for "strangers" also God has made provision in the new temple. "The sons of strangers shall build up thy walls." Their gifts, like those of the people of Tyre, shall help to rear and adorn them. "If they come and pray in this house, then hear thou from the heavens, even from thy dwelling-place, and do according to all that the

---

* Luke vi. 20.

† Dr. J. I. DOLLINGER, *The First Age of Christianity and the Church*, vol. ii., p. 239, says, with great truth, "Nearly all the first converts were from the poorer and humbler classes. The only known exceptions are Nicodemus, Joseph, Sergius Paulus, Diony-sius the Areopagite, Apollos and Paul himself. That was the order of Christianity—first came the poor, the ignorant and uneducated slaves and the very lowest classes. Gradually, and after a long interval, the powerful, the wise, the rich were won by them, or rather were overcome and compelled to follow in the general movement."

stranger calleth to thee for, that all people of the earth may know thy name and fear thee." The gifts of even such as are "strangers to the covenants of promise" are due from them, as creatures of God's hand and care. Such men and women in our churches, who honor Christ by gifts and labors with sincere hearts and seeking his grace, often find, as Solomon says, that "a man's gift maketh room for him, and bringeth him before" the King. The enlistment of unconverted persons in deeds of charity, and contributions for the work of the Church, powerfully helps to bring them and Christ into one—not of their merit, for they owe him all things, but of his grace.*

SHOULD THE MINISTRY BE GOVERNED BY THE APOSTLE'S RULE OF GIVING.

Shall the ministry of the gospel give according to the apostolic rule?—is an important question as to which many desire to have their minds at rest.

Such matters must be determined by the knowledge and conscience of each one for himself. We are ministers of God; and "every one of us shall give account of *himself* to God." But the following considerations may help some in ascertaining the way of duty.

The Levites, under the former Dispensation, were instructed by Moses to give of all the tithes which the people paid to themselves a tenth to the high priest.† The high priest was the type of him who is set on the right hand of the majesty in the heavens, the honor of whose service, and the

* Isa. lx. 10.   2 Chron. xi. 33.   Prov. xviii. 16.
† Ex. xxx. 11–16.

preciousness of whose name in all the earth, surely claim an equal measure of consecration from his ministering brethren. Can we do less for our Jesus than the Levite did for Aaron, or Samuel, or Abiathar?

Our Lord Jesus Christ paid the didrachma, or half-shekel of the sanctuary, for himself and Peter, when it was asked of them; and wrought a miracle for the purpose, bringing it by the mouth of a fish. Olshausen says,* "The question put by the collectors of this assessment, whether Jesus would pay it, assuredly arose from the circumstance of these persons believing that as a theocratic teacher he would regard himself as free from such an impost. But Peter, to whom the question was addressed in the absence of Jesus, believed, that with his strong religious feelings, he would make it a point to pay such holy taxes, and answered affirmatively." "The Lord's words at the same time clearly prove that Jesus acknowledged and honored the Old Testament order in general as a Divine institute." "He contemplated the whole temple service in its preparatory character." It was spiritualized by Christ's death. Trench observes† that, "the word 'tribute' in our translation upholds an error, and leads men's thoughts in the wrong direction—to consider this a civil impost, instead of what it truly was, a theocratic payment, due to the temple and the temple's God."

The apostles and first ministry of the gospel as they freely

* Comments, on the Gospels; Part III. BLOOMFIELD; Recensio Synoptica, says, "I entirely agree with those who tell us that this was the sacred tribute, the half shekel." Ex. xxx. 11–16. JACOBUS, Notes on Matthew, is to the same effect.

† TRENCH; Notes on the Miracles, 299–311.

13

received, did freely give.   Paul wrought with his own hands as a tent-maker; others as fishermen, to minister to their own necessities, and those also of their fellow-laborers.   We are told that Barnabas, or Joses, who had been a Levite, and became one of the most faithful ministers of the Christian Church, sold his entire possessions and brought the money and laid it for distribution at the apostle's feet.

The personal power of the ministry of the gospel must be based upon the mutual sympathy of pastors and people. The pastor must be willing to be " tempted in all points like as they are," and the severest of their temptations in this evil world are, as a whole, those which spring from trials connected with money.   The affections of the people are powerfully drawn out toward a pastor who is beneficent in the use of money.

Continual efforts to obtain money from a people without the personal example of liberality, creates irritation and hostility.   If the ministry do not exercise corresponding care to cultivate their own grace of giving, the ordinary result has ever been to generate in themselves and their order covetousness, pride, strifes, and hierarchical assumptions.

Wisdom, economy and forethought are necessary in the affairs of ministers, as of other men.   Yet the most certain provision which a minister can make for his old age and for the care of his family is *not* in saving and hoarding a portion of his income, at the expense of liberality.   It is wise in him to educate, by his example and spirit, hundreds of families to generosity and sympathy.   They become to him more than brothers and sisters.   Such a man when old is rarely forsaken, nor do his seed beg bread.   There is a great secret of Divine Providence just in this method of making a man's loss become "an hundred fold" gain to him and to his children after him.

Personal comfort, assurance of God's love, peace of conscience, joy in the Holy Ghost, and increase of every grace, peculiarly flow from liberal systematic charity; and the minister who from true love to God and man gives abundantly will find that when his knowledge and learning, when his earthly faith and hope and their exercise, shall cease, this "shall abide" in its eternal and joyful rewards.

The amount of money which a definite proportion of the incomes of the ministry alone would afford, to aid the work of the Church, far surpasses the imagination of most persons. The salaries of the near five thousand ministers of the Presbyterian Church amount to about four millions of dollars per annum.* The one tenth of this sum would be equal to the present total average contributions of the whole Church to the foreign or home mission boards. If distributed among the several boards it would support one-fourth of their entire work. We know, however, that the contributions of the ministry form a large part of the present revenues of the boards, and are proportionally greatly in advance of those of the laity.

---

* In the years 1872 and 1873 the salaries were reported to the General Assembly. They amounted, so far as given, to $2,597,342, for 4,441 men, in the one year; and $3,151,767, for 4,534 men, in the other. Adding ministers and even entire presbyteries not responding then to the call, and also other sources of income from which most ministers would no doubt desire to add offerings to God, the amount would appear to not be under what is named.

The example is still more powerful than the precepts of the minister who contributes liberally to the claims which he advocates. His preaching of the gospel obtains a new hold upon the respect of his hearers. We observe in the general history of churches that an extraordinary blessing has seemed to follow the labors of men who have made the exercise of liberality a regular and prominent feature of their ministry. Some of them, as Isaac Watts, and John Wesley, and George Whitfield, have instituted mighty influences which have revolutionized the spirit of great bodies of Christians.

The present era is a general " time of re-formation," the "fullness of times," which has had no parallel since the Levitical dispensation passed away, and old things passed away and all things became new amidst the joys of Christ's coming to make full atonement for sin. Now he comes to reign. Our brethren of that previous era were made " a spectacle unto the world, and to angels, and to men." They suffered hunger and thirst and nakedness; they were buffeted; they labored, working with their own hands; they were reviled, persecuted, defamed; they were made the filth of all things, and the offscouring of the world. Thus, they filled up that which is behind of the afflictions of Christ, for his body's sake, which is the Church. Have *we* no cross to bear? Is he not to be glorified *now* by a " witness"— "if needs be," a martyrdom—of suffering? Or is it only a few who are called to deny themselves?

> " Must Jesus bear the cross alone,
> And all the world go free?
> No! there's a cross for every one,
> And there's a cross for me."

How little can we do for him, compared with what he did, and does, and promises for us! But this let us do, until his gospel is "preached to every creature which is under heaven;" "striving according to his working, which worketh in us mightily." *

Such are the considerations which have moved many of our ministers to adopt the rule of laying by some proportionate part, generally not less than one tenth, of their income, for contributions to the work of the Church through her boards and to such claims as may arise within the sphere of their own observation. The general character of the Presbyterian and Protestant ministry suggests the probability that the practice of that which seems to be so thoroughly approved by Scripture, by reason, by experience, and by its fruits, will become universal, and "every one" of the tribe of Levi, also, in this latter day, lay by of his means as God has prospered.

* Heb. ix. 10. Eph. i. 10. 1 Cor. iv. 9–13. Col. i. 23–29.

CHAPTER X.

THE POWER OF UNIVERSAL COMBINATION.

IT is the purpose of the divine rule to do more than merely engage every *class* in the Church in giving. It aims to enlist every single individual; and to give him, or her, a place and a share in the work of bringing the world into obedience to the Lord Jesus Christ. It would make him the Head of a body which has not in it a single dead or useless member.

The power of the Church of Christ, were this idea brought into effect in regard to pecuniary contributions, can be best understood by observing the applications of the principle in the affairs of the world.

EFFECT IN SUPPORTING A NATIONAL POSTAL SYSTEM.

There was a day, not longer ago than that in which the foundations of European civilization were laid by the Roman empire, when the cost of sending a letter a couple of thousand miles may be rated at many thousands of dollars of our money. It implied some great necessity or privilege, the employment of courageous and experienced couriers, expensive relays of horses, the protection of armed soldiery, and great perils from savage races, wild beasts, storms, floods and accidents.

Now, a sealed letter is sent, in America, from St. Augustine in Florida to New Archangel in Alaska for three cents; or a postal card or a newspaper for one cent. The distance is more than twice as great, the persons employed more numerous, the total expense far greater. Why the difference in the cost of transmission?

It is because in the former case few letters were sent, and they upon affairs of the government, or between persons of rank or importance. In the latter case, the entire population, scarcely a family excepted, employs the mails. Some individuals write hundreds of letters, and some send forth thousands, or even tens of thousands, of circulars during the year. Hence, without counting regular newspaper and magazine postage, the adhesive stamps annually used sum up from six to seven hundred millions. This universal employment of the mails supports a vast system of nearly ten thousand mail-routes, which connect together all the cities, towns and hamlets of the immense territory of the nation; their aggregate length is ten times the circumference of the globe, and that of the separate trips of the mails upon them is greater by one third than the distance from the earth to the sun—near a hundred and thirty millions of miles. The expense of this stupendous machinery, which employs, in numerous ways, many thousands of men, is from thirty to thirty-five millions of dollars a year.

No lesson could be more impressive than this one as to the incalculable importance of the universal combination of a people to accomplish a great object.

SUCCESS OF FRENCH POPULAR LOANS.

The European wars of a few centuries ago were carried on at terrible disadvantage on account of the difficulty of obtaining money. It was secured by forced loans from subjects, by oppressive and unequal taxes and imposts, by despotic confiscations of property, and other pernicious means.

The extraordinary financial ability of the late emperor Louis Napoleon brought into operation in France a system of popular loans which accomplished results that were looked upon by the financiers of the world with astonishment. The Rothschilds and other capitalists having declined to furnish him with money for the prosecution of the Crimean war, on satisfactory terms, he threw himself upon the people. The success of the measure was so great that five principal loans were effected, in the years 1854 to 1864, for the support of that and the subsequent Italian war, and for the consolidation of floating debts. The amount asked for in them was about four hundred millions of dollars (2,052,250,000 francs); the subscriptions offered were for two thousand and seven hundred millions of dollars (13,694,034,888 francs); that is, for nearly *seven times* the sum needed. The number of separate subscriptions, in sums varying chiefly from ten dollars to two thousand, and many of them payable in monthly instalments, was 1,828,951. This financial triumph accomplished for Louis Napoleon some other very important ends, not the least of which was the firmer establishment for the time of his throne upon the interests and regards of the common people of France, since one third of the six millions of the families of the country, instead of counting the war a burthen, became directly concerned in its success, and in the measures which were necessary to produce it.

FINANCIAL LESSONS OF OUR CIVIL WAR.

During the late civil war, our own nation learned a lessou from the example of the French loans, which has affected our whole political and financial history.   At the beginning of the war the appalling problem of the government was that of the procuring of money to carry it on.   Foreign help and friendship failed us, and the nation without this vital instrumentality must have perished.   The financial abilities and experience of Mr. Jay Cooke were put in requisition. He appealed to the resources and loyalty of the people themselves, assured that this was the only hope of the government, and that it would not fail him.   A series of popular loans was instituted.   Bonds, even of small amounts, and compound interest notes, were made accessible to the whole population; their patriotism and sympathies were appealed to; abundant information was disseminated in the newspapers, and by circulars and pamphlets; and *every man* was solicited to help in this way, according to his means, in the great struggle for national life.   The result was, that in eighteen months Mr. Cooke funded five hundred millions of dollars in "five-twenties;" and this was done at an expense, including commissions of agents, of only one-half of one per cent.   No European loan was ever made so cheaply. In August, 1864, the "seven-thirty loan" was brought out, but proved a failure.   In February, 1865, it was put in Mr.

Cooke's hands. He employed the same methods as before, and appealed to the people for support. One of his first acts was to put seventy-five thousand dollars' worth of advertisements into the newspapers. This effort, in turn, was so surprisingly successful, notwithstanding the enormous drains of the war in different ways upon the people, that by July, or in only five months, he had sold seven hundred millions of dollars' worth of the bonds and closed the loan.

The lessons which these appeals to the entire people of the country taught the government and the financiers were of indescribable importance. It was these small contributions from hundreds of thousands of farmers, working men, women, people who felt that the bond was their "*substitute*" in the fight, which saved the country. And while this revenue equipped our armies and fleets, provided for the sick and disabled, and carried on this gigantic war, it did far more; it enlisted under the national banner the men and women, and even the children, of the whole nation; it annihilated the old distinctions of party; it warmed the whole population with a new love of country and appreciation of the value of its institutions; it braced us up with a courage and sound national self-respect which we had never before possessed; it developed our vast manufacturing, mineral, and general productive wealth, to an astonishing degree; it left us not as we feared crushed, bankrupt, and ruined, but absolutely twice as rich nationally as we were before the war commenced. It was a grand national realization of how *blessed* it is for "every one" *to give.*   .

We conceive it to be almost impossible that this stupendous lesson, which God in the wondrous methods of his providence set before the eyes of his Church in this nation, holding it up before our reluctant and weeping eyes, and laying the rod upon us all the while, can be lost. But if it accomplish not its object—if we do not put in operation the practicable means for enlisting the entire population of the Church, its men, its women, and its children, in the desperate war to rescue immortal souls from the power and curse and woes of sin to crush the resistance of hell to the glorious kingdom of the Lord Jesus Christ, and to fill the nation and the world with the beneficent triumphs of the gospel of his grace—then assuredly we do deserve more and severer chastisement. And we will receive it.

Evils of Partial Methods of Contribution.

The pernicious effects of the opposite methods of obtaining the means necessary for the support of the State are so great, that they have gradually fallen into disuse on the part of monarchical governments, and have been rejected, save in a few and extreme cases in our own. The arbitrary and unequal assessments upon individuals, or classes, or guilds, or towns, or commercial companies; the granting of monopolies of the trade or manufacture of particular articles, or of commercial traffic with certain foreign countries; the farming of the taxes upon the people of certain districts for a given sum of money; all such things in the past, among our ancestry, we read of with a sort of horror. We bless God for the men who resisted and overthrew them, sometimes at the sacrifice of their own fortunes and lives. We are grateful that we have experienced so few of such evils under our republican institutions.

Income taxes, which are usually fixed at five or ten per cent. upon incomes of over a certain amount, may be classed among the measures of this nature. A tax of this character upon incomes of over six hundred dollars, with certain deductions allowed upon the excess, was laid upon our country during the severe trials of the civil war. It was exceedingly odious. Its influence upon the moral tone of society was very injurious. Hundreds of thousands evaded it. It led to much dishonesty and falsehood. It realized about fifty millions of dollars in the year after the close of the war, which was assessed upon only four hundred and sixty thousand persons. This sunk to under thirty-five millions in 1869. The tax was dropped in 1870. Mr. J. Stuart Mill says, in his "Political Economy,"* of such taxes, "To tax the larger incomes at a higher per centage than the smaller, is to lay a tax on industry and economy; to impose a penalty on people for having worked harder and saved more than their neighbors. It is partial taxation, which is a mild form of robbery." "I can hardly conceive a more shameless pretension than that the major part of the property of the country [which would not be within the sphere of such an assessment] should be exempted from its share of taxation."

The lesson from the experiences of the State should here again be laid to heart by the Church. The same evils flow from arbitrary and unequal requirements in this case as in that. The demands upon certain communities, and upon certain men who have obtained a name for liberality, have been felt by them to be oppressive. It has led to resistance

* Book vi., chap. ii.

on their part. They have characterized it as "a *partial*
taxation," unequal and unfair. The time has come for the
adoption by the Church of an equitable system of voluntary contributions by the people, one in accordance with
Scripture, which will enable her to, enlist the aid of all her
membership, in proportion to their means; and this not
alone to bear the light burdens of the past, but to supply
the immeasurably greater demands of the conflicts before
her.

Evidence from the Success of Methodism.

So recent was the rise of Episcopal Methodism, that there
are many men and women alive who were born in the life-
time of its founder, John Wesley. It was in 1739 that,
after a stormy interview at Lambeth with the archbishop of
Canterbury, in which His Grace threatened him with excommunication for field preaching, Wesley determined to
"break down the bridge" which connected him with the
power of the Established Church, and "fight his way forward." He began, in preaching to the populace at Moor-
fields and the colliers at Kingwood, an "itinerant" career
which ended in 1791.

The fact seems almost incredible that to-day this still
youthful Church and its offshoots number four millions of
members, over three millions of whom are in the United
States, and that it has a total leadership of twenty-five
thousand itinerant or regular preachers, and sixty-three
thousand local preachers. The "Methodist Episcopal
Church" (of the North) alone, which contains one million
and a half of members, gives seventeen and a half millions

of dollars to religious and charitable objects. The property of the several Methodist bodies stood far above that of any other Church in value, in the national census of 1870, amounting to within a fraction of seventy millions of dollars.

What is the cause of this truly amazing growth? We have it in the famous watchword of all its members: "Justification, sanctification, and a penny a week." First, faith in Jesus Christ alone for salvation; second, personal holiness, complete consecration to God through the Spirit; third, universal weekly giving through the Church of at least one penny for every member. As to this first point, their knowledge of the principles of faith is notoriously deficient; as to the second, their spirituality is deformed with excesses of mere physical excitement; as to the third, they have not reached the application of more than a part of the mighty Divine Rule of Paul. And yet there stand the solid and sublime evidences of their astonishing success in doing the work of building up both the spiritual and the material walls of the temple of Christ.

The engagement of the "lay-members" of the Church in active work, and contributions for its maintenance, is a principal element of the Methodist success. There are enumerated in the ecclesiastical reports those filling various offices. Thus, in the Church North, to which allusion has been made, there are fifty-four thousand class-leaders, eighty-seven thousand stewards of societies, one hundred and two thousand trustees of churches, twenty-five thousand sunday-school superintendents, and one hundred and seventy-eight thousand teachers and other officers of sunday-schools.

The peculiar organization which has given to Episcopal

Methodism its chief power is that of the "classes." Their origin and nature are worthy of careful study. The following is the account of their origin as given by Richard Watson, the biographer of the Rev. John Wesley.*

"In the discipline of Methodism the division of the society into classes is an important branch. Each class is placed under a person of experience and piety, who meets the others once a week for prayers and inquiry into the religious state of each, in order to administer exhortation and counsel." The origin of the classes is thus traced out. "The chapel in Bristol was in debt, and it was agreed that each member of the society should contribute one penny a week to reduce the burden. The Bristol society was therefore divided into classes, and for convenience one person was appointed to collect weekly subscriptions from each class, and to pay the amount to the stewards. The advantages of this system, when turned to a higher purpose, at once struck the methodical and practical mind of Mr. Wesley. He therefore invited several 'earnest and sensible men' to meet him, and the society in London was divided into classes like that of Bristol, and placed under the spiritual care of these tried and experienced persons. At first they visited each person at his own residence once a week, but the preferable mode of bringing each class together weekly was at length adopted. . . . Opportunities were also thus afforded for ascertaining the wants of the poorer members, and obtaining relief for them, and for visiting the sick: the duty of a leader being to see his members once in the week, either at the meeting, or, if absent from that, at home."

* *Life of Wesley*, chap. vii.

Mr. Wesley remarks in his Journal with regard to these "classes," which had been organized as the most "methodical" and practical way of spreading the gospel and building up the Church: "Upon reflection, I could not but observe, *this is the very thing which was from the beginning of Christianity.* In the earliest times, those whom God had sent forth 'preached the gospel to every creature.' The body of the hearers were mostly either Jews or heathen.   But as soon as any of these were so convinced of the truth as to forsake sin, and seek the gospel of salvation, they immediately joined them together, took an account of their names, advised them to watch over each other, and met these 'catechumens,' as they were then called, apart from the great congregation, that they might instruct, rebuke, exhort, and pray with them, and for them, according to their several necessities."

To complete and make more efficacious the work of the classes, Mr. Wesley afterward, beginning in London, appointed "visitors to the sick." They were to visit them thrice a week, advise them spiritually, relieve their wants, furnish them with medical care, and bring in their accounts weekly to the stewards. Mr. Wesley says: "Upon reflection, I saw how exactly in this also we copied after the Primitive Church.   What were the ancient deacons?   What was Phebe, the deaconess, but such a visitor of the sick?"

It is in place to notice here that the instructions in the "Discipline" of the "Methodist Episcopal Church" in the United States, for the guidance of its class-leaders, are as follows:* "That it may the more easily be discerned

* Chap. ii., section 1.

whether they are indeed working out their own salvation, each society is divided into smaller companies, called classes, according to their respective places of abode. There are about twelve persons in a class, one of whom is styled the leader. It is his duty, I. To see each person in his class once a week at least, in order, 1. To inquire how their souls prosper. 2. To advise, reprove, comfort or exhort, as occasion may require. 3. To receive what they are willing to give toward the relief of the preachers, church, and poor. II. To meet the ministers and the stewards of the society once a week, in order, 1. To inform the minister of any that are sick, or of any that walk disorderly and will not be reproved. 2. To pay the stewards what they have received of their several classes in the week preceding."

In the organization of the Methodists for Christian purposes we have the evidence of the extraordinary abilities, for such an end, of the leading mind which gave its impress to the whole Church. The opinion of Isaac Taylor was that, "In dealing with whatever may belong to a process of organization, or of marshaling a host for a single initiatory purpose, Wesley has never been surpassed by civil, military, or ecclesiastical mechanists."

The power of Methodism is traced by this vigorous thinker, on the one hand, to the convictions of personal responsibility to God which it fixed in the hearts of its members. He says, "It was the proper consequence of the Methodistic preaching to call into activity that life of the soul, as individually related to God, which must be named as one of its distinctive elements." But this individual faith and zeal must, on the other hand, be associated, as are the different

14

members of one frame, for co-operation to a great common end.   Here its power is exhibited in its assigning to "*every one*" a suitable part to perform.   Mr. Taylor therefore presents this strongly to view.   He says : "An organization which touches every one, and brings every one into his place, and exacts from every one his contribution, spiritual and secular—an organization which is comprehensive in the most absolute sense as to persons, gifts, talents, and worldly means—is that which has secured for Wesleyan Methodism, until of late, its foremost place among the Protestant communities of England and America, and which has given to its labors among the heathen a proportionally greater amount of success than has attended the equally zealous endeavors of other bodies, perhaps of several such bodies reckoned together."   It "has proved itself hitherto the most efficient expansive Christian institute which modern times have seen ; it must be presumed, therefore, to possess excellence of structure of a very peculiar kind, and which should command the attention of all who make ecclesiastical economics their study." *

That which is most conspicuous and impressive in Wesleyan Methodism is, that its peculiar features of power and excellence are all the modern reproduction of those of the Primitive Christian Church.   They were seized upon instinctively, from the Scriptures and church history, by a comprehensive, powerful and practical mind like Wesley's, guided by the enlightening influence of the Holy Spirit. The fervent preaching of salvation through Christ, the duty of seeking personal holiness, the inspiration of the joyful

* Isaac Taylor; *Wesley and Methodism,* pp. 79, 158, 249, 696.

hymns, the cordial fellowship, the sympathy with and provision for the poor, the urging of individual accountability,
the general co-operation in good works, the weekly contributions of money, the continual official employment of male
and female members in charitable duties, all are elements
which are reflections, in this great revival from the formalism of a century ago in England, which come directly from
Primitive Christianity.

POSSIBLE POWER OF A CHURCH COMBINING THESE
CHARACTERISTICS WITH OTHERS MORE THOROUGHLY
SCRIPTURAL.

Let us suppose a Church in which these characteristics are
combined with a thoroughly scriptural theology, with more
intelligent instruction, with more judicious discipline,* and
with a broader comprehension of the principles of pecuniary
giving—above all, let it be animated thoroughly with glowing
love to Jesus Christ, let it be energized by the influences of
the Holy Spirit of God—and it needs no tongue of a prophet
to declare that such a Christianity would be more powerful
than even that of the first centuries; for now it has general
advantages and instrumentalities far greater than those of
the Primitive Church.   It would in a brief time literally
and truly conquer the whole world, and bring it into loving
obedience to its glorious and rightful Lord.

* It was found upon careful examination of its statistics, from the
year 1855 to 1865, that but one in six of those entered as "proba-
tioners" became "members" of the Methodist Church.

CHAPTER XI.

THE CULTIVATION OF PERSONAL CHARACTER.

THE fame of no one of the preachers of the gospel in the early centuries of Christianity stands so high for eloquence as that of John Chrysostom. Such was its power that on many occasions the excited audiences at Antioch and Constantinople burst forth in acts of loud applause. Notwithstanding the severity, with which he rebuked their sins, they emptied the places of public resort and excitement to crowd, in the latter city, the great church of St. Sophia. He roused them to a surprising degree of liberality, for the building of institutions of charity and for sending forth evangelists to Asia Minor, Persia, Scythia and other regions which had not yet received the gospel. And yet the example of the freedom with which he poured out in acts of liberality his own fortune, which he had inherited from his parents, incited them still more than his burning words.*

---

* John, who was afterward surnamed Chrysostom, or, for his eloquence, the "golden-mouthed," was born at Antioch, about the year 347. His father, Secundus, was a Roman military officer, who died while this child was a young infant. His education, training and character he owed to his mother Anthusa, who remained a widow that she might satisfactorily perform her duties to her son. It was in regard to her that the celebrated teacher Libanius made the ex-

THE PRIESTHOOD OF THE CHRISTIAN.

Taking up the idea that Christian offerings to God on the Sabbath are the noblest evidence of their priesthood, he thus paints the honor of it. To make these offerings, says he, "constituteth them priests: yea, of a priesthood which bringeth great reward. The merciful man is not arrayed in a robe reaching to the feet, nor does he put on bells, nor wear a crown. But he is wrapped in a robe of loving kindness, a holier than the sacerdotal vestments. He is anointed with oil, not formed of material elements, but compounded by the Holy Spirit. He weareth a crown of mercies, for it is declared, 'He crowneth thee with loving kindness and tender mercies.' Instead of wearing upon it a plate inscribed with the name of God, he is in himself like unto God. In what way? Because it is said, 'Ye shall be like unto your Father which is in heaven.'"

In commenting upon the Christian Rule for Giving, Chrysostom sheds a most important light upon the understanding of its requirements which prevailed in the East at that day. The following are his remarks upon the words "lay by him

clamation, "What wives these Christians have!" The Church historian THEODORET; *Ec. Hist.*, V. xxvii., styles Chrysostom "the great luminary of the world." He was, there is no doubt, misled by his devout aspirations, in an age when he had not the guidance of the Church's subsequent experience, into asceticism; he was severe and sometimes imperious. Yet he deserves the admiring testimony of NEANDER (*Pref.* to First ed. of *Life of Chrysostom*), who says, "None of the ancient Fathers have laid down so many truths of practical importance, and so equally suited to all ages, as Chrysostom."

in store." The apostle "does not say, 'let him bring it into the Church,' lest they might feel ashamed of the sum; but, 'having by gradual additions swelled his contribution, let him produce it when I come.' Therefore 'for the present, lay it up,' says he, 'at home, and make thine own house a church, and thy little box a treasury.' Become thyself a guardian of consecrated wealth, a self-ordained steward of the poor. Thy charitable mind entitles thee to this priesthood." "Let us make a little chest for the poor at home. Near the place at which you stand praying, there let it be put; and as often as you enter in to pray, first deposit your alms, and then send up your prayer. You would not wish to pray with unclean hands, so neither do it without alms." "If you have this little treasury, you have a defence against the devil. You give wings to your prayer. You make your house sacred, having provision for the King laid up there in store."*

INTERPRETATION OF THE RULE.

These passages most happily and clearly present to us the general method and principles of the religious contributions of Christians in the early centuries of the Church. They come to us from one who labored in the great centre of the missionary efforts of the Apostolic Church: of which, indeed, òn account of their zeal, it is recorded in the book of Acts, that "the disciples were called *Christians* first in Antioch." † This light shows to us the meaning of those words in the divine rule ‡ which our common version trans-

---

* *Homilies*, 1 *Cor.*; XLIII.   † Chap. xi. 26.

‡ παρ ἑαυτῷ τιθέτω θησαυρίζων.

lates "lay by him in store." They may be literally rendered, "let each of you *by himself set apart, treasuring,*
whatsoever he has prospered in." There are two distinct
verbs in the original; one directing the setting apart of the
money given, the other the treasuring of it, or putting it into
such treasuries, private or public, as were needed to secure
it for the use of the officers of the Church.

The verb translated "lay by," or "set apart," is one
which often has a formal meaning: to *commit, appoint,*
constitute, ordain. Thus it is said: "take heed to the flock
over the which the Holy Ghost *hath made* you overseers."
God "*hath committed* unto us the word of reconciliation."
"As many as were possessors of lands or houses sold them,
and brought the prices of the things that were sold, and
laid them *down* at the apostles feet." "I have chosen
you and *ordained* you, that ye should go and bring forth
fruit."*

The verb "treasuring," which our version renders, for
the sake of simplicity, "in store," means making a particular deposit, or distinct accumulation. Thus, "*lay* not *up* for
yourselves *treasures* upon earth." "So is he that *layeth*
up treasure for himself, and is not rich toward God." "Ye
have heaped together treasure for the last days." "*Treasur-*
eth up unto thyself wrath against the day of wrath." So
with the corresponding noun; as in the words, "*treasure* hid
in a field." † The participle is used, apparently, to generalize
the idea, and allow liberty in respect to the localities, or

---

* Acts xx. 28; v. 19.   2 Cor. v. 19.

† Mal. vi. 19.   Luke xii. 21.   James v. 3.   Rom. ii. 5.   Matt.
xiii. 44.

depositories, or forms, in which the money or other contributions are to be kept.   Only they are to be "treasured
apart."

The preposition and noun translated "by him" are really
more emphatic; they are literally "by himself."   "By"
means "beside, near," and is a preposition of *place;* yet
sometimes with the broader idea of property in general.
The words "by himself" are often idiomatic in the Greek,
and mean "near himself *at home;*"* the "treasuring"
should first be "on the first day of the week," as a regular
duty *at home.*   Yet the word "treasuring" implies that the
worshiper may put the sums accumulated into the public
depository of the church, when convenient for preservation,
security, or use in such ways as he may designate.

The first and most solemn transaction then manifestly was
the *private* "setting apart," dedication and consecration of
a share of a man's income to the Lord.   This was a duty
which belonged to the business of every week, and the con-

---

* In regard to this very important practical point it is designed
that the explanations shall convey the sense of the best interpreters,
ancient and modern.   The Syriac translation renders the words
"by him" as meaning *at home.*   The later Hebrew New Testament,
separate *alone,* as in Gen. xxxii. 25, and Ex. xviii. 14.   The Latin
Vulgate, " apud se seponat ;" " apud se" was an idiomatic expression
for "the dwelling, the house of a person."   ANDREWS' *Lat. Lex.*
The French, "*mette à part chez soi,*" which is the same idiom.   The
German, "*lege bei sich selbst.*"   JOSEPHUS, *Antiq.* xx. 10, uses the
words (παρ ἑαυτῶ) which are here translated "by him" interchange-
ably with another word (οικαδε) which means "at one's house, or
home."   Most of the ancient and modern commentators strongly
emphasize this feature of the Rule.

secration of it unto God to every Sabbath : though the *public* act of presenting it could be performed when suitable occasions were offered. Tertullian says "each one makes a contribution on a certain day, or when he chooses." They were sometimes handed in to the church "once a month." This private consecration is the imitation of the picture presented to us in the discourse of Chrysostom.

LEADING OBJECT, TO ENLIST PRAYER.

To enlist prayer for the objects to which money is given is, no doubt, God's first purpose in requiring the private setting apart of contributions each Sabbath. This is most manifest to one who has observed the spirit of the passage in the original Scripture. It is to be solemnly and prayerfully set apart and dedicated to God's service. Prayers go to the throne of universal dominion. God, in answer to them, sets in motion the ministering hosts which are invisible to mortal eyes. Our money and labors belong to the lower machinery of earth ; prayer sets in action those living spirits within the wheels which Ezekiel saw in his vision. "When those went, these went; and when those stood, these stood." Material agencies of providence have no life or power save as they are thus animated from on high ; and as they are directed by that "voice" which the prophet heard from the sapphire throne upon which was One having "the appearance of a man."*

This is the spirit of the instruction of Jesus Christ in the sermon on the mount. He enjoins as to alms and prayer, that they be "in secret," and "thy Father which seeth in

* Ezek. ch. i.

secret himself shall reward thee openly." The whole Bible is full of precepts which bind them together.

The first desire and prayer of every one that gives should be that his offering may be "an odor of a sweet smell, a sacrifice acceptable, well-pleasing to God," who "shall supply all your need according to his riches in glory by Christ Jesus." Our liberality and self-denial for his sake will be repaid "an hundred fold" if accepted in heaven; "for with such sacrifices God is well pleased." John saw in the last judgment that "the books were opened" in which are recorded all that we have done for Christ, and "the dead were judged out of those things which were written in the books, according to their works." *

But there is a far more important reason for our accompanying every gift of money with prayer: many may be saved thereby. The man whom God was pleased to accept as the first fruits of the harvest from among the Gentiles was thus honored because he "gave much alms to the people, and prayed to God always." The angel of God said unto him, "Cornelius, thy prayer is heard, and thine alms are had in remembrance in the sight of God;" and an apostle was sent to him and to his kinsfolk and near friends, with gracious tidings of salvation.† In public worship, and in secret exercises, we should follow prayer by alms as the means of its fulfillment. Prayer should be *sealed*, in pleading with a covenant-keeping God, by alms; in all nations a contract is not counted valid till it be sealed with a payment of money. Alms should be made potent and successful in their design by prayer. What multitudes would be con-

* Phil. iv. 18, 19. Rev. xx. 12.   † Acts x.

verted to-day, in this and that dark and unpromising field at home, or abroad, if each dollar which is sent thither were followed by "the effectual fervent prayer" of the giver for God's Holy Spirit to follow its appropriation with blessings upon the labors of the preacher, the teacher, the physician, the Bible or tract distributor. The seed of the word, wherever planted, must be steeped in prayers and tears to make it bring forth abundantly.

BENEFICENCE A REGULAR PRINCIPLE OF THE CHRISTIAN LIFE.

Another of God's great designs in appointing this private setting apart was, doubtless, that beneficence should be made a habitual principle of the life of every Christian.

Mr. Barnes, in his explanation of the Divine Rule, presses strongly this feature of it. He says,* "'Let him set it apart.' Let him designate a certain portion; let him do this '*by himself*,' when he is at home, when he can calmly look at the evidence of his prosperity. Let him do it not under the influence of pathetic appeals, or for the sake of display when he is with others, but let him do it as a matter of principle, and when he is by himself." "Paul designed that the habit of doing good with their money should be constant. He therefore directed that it should be on the return of each Lord's day, so that the subject should be constantly before their minds. How much would the amount of charities be swelled in the Christian Church if all Christians would lay by in store each week what they then could devote to sacred purposes."

* *Notes on First Corinthians.*

The Divine Rule cultivates individual giving from princi-ple. *Regularity* in giving is like regularity in eating. It is healthful; the digestion is easy, and every organ of the frame is invigorated; the growth and development of the powers is continuous; the effects are good success, and gen-uine enjoyment and comfort, in whatever work employs our thoughts and strength.

The opposite kind of giving is that which has made our "Voluntary System" objectionable in the eyes of Christians of other lands. Our system, it is to be hoped, will ever be "voluntary," as not being compulsory by any State, or ecclesiastical enactments. But it certainly should not be spontaneous or spasmodic.

"Spontaneous" is an adjective which is defined to mean that which proceeds from natural feeling or impulse, with-out consideration, that which is produced without being planted, or without cultivation. Spontaneous giving has numerous essential and vital defects. Its products are some-times abundant and beautiful; but they depend upon contin-gencies of soil, and exposure, and want of cultivation, which make them unreliable in any one season or year. The con-gregations, or men, that give in this way, suffer from a sort of religious epilepsy. To-day they are in spasms and fever, foaming and uncontrollable; to-morrow the fit is off, and they are exhausted, fretful or stupid, incapable of work. And this last state may be long protracted.

The general effect of benevolent work carried on by ap-peals to this kind of charity, is most unfavorable to its reg-ular and healthful development. It sometimes manifests a certain temporary energetic activity. Its spirit, however.

is material and sensational.   Material interests, politics, calamities, accidents, new agents, new measures, local or occasional public excitements, are its natural themes.   Even the spiritual experiences and hopes of the Church and of men's souls must be displayed in a sentimental and pretentious manner, which is offensive and painful to genuine feeling.   Neglect of careful instruction, levity of manner, coarse illustrations, creep into the pulpit.   The lust of excitement is kindled in the people.   The mighty spiritual motives of the gospel evaporate, and the omnipotent co-operation of the Holy Ghost is defeated, as the fertilizing dews of Hermon and Lebanon are dried up by a hot east wind from the deserts of Moab.

EVERY KIND OF EMPLOYMENT TO BE SPIRITUALIZED.

It is a grand object of the Divine Rule to infuse spiritual motives into all the ordinary employments of men's hands and time.

The duty of giving is taken up by Paul a second time, in another epistle to the Corinthians.*   The apostle in this treats chiefly of the spiritual motives which should impel liberality—the grace of our Lord Jesus Christ; the example of it in churches which abounded in it even amidst a great trial of affliction, and their joy in it; the lessons of that divine providence which, as in sending the manna of old, will ever supply sufficiently our wants; the necessity of seeking and cultivating liberality as "a grace," just as we do knowledge, faith, utterance, and all diligence; and the assurance of proportionate returns for our faithfulness, just

---

* Chaps. viii. and ix.

as the industry of the sower ministers food and multiplies bread. "Bountifulness" is part of a spiritual industry by which we are "enriched in everything."

The word "righteousness" is used by Paul in a sense which is foreign to our modes of thought. He quotes from the Old Testament: "As it is written, he hath dispersed abroad; he hath given to the poor; his righteousness remaineth for ever."* The word means conformity to duty and right. *We* call practical charity "benevolence," and "beneficence;" just as if its exercise were a matter of choice and of merit. *He* makes it a "right" of Christianity—a law, like "the law of kindness" which king Lemuel† says governs the family of the virtuous woman—a law, albeit a "law of love." In Eastern nations, where we say "charitable" they often say "righteous." One sees, for instance, over the door of what we entitle a "Charity School," out of which are flocking the children of the poor, and which is supported by the contributions of those whom God has more abundantly favored, the remarkable inscription "RIGHTEOUS SCHOOL." In illustrating the duty of giving, Paul says of the Macedonians, "they first gave their own selves to the Lord, and unto us by the will of God." Thus, like faithful bondmen to Christ and his kingdom, "beyond their power they were willing" to give the proceeds of their labor to him and for his service.

Every kind of business and employment is to be spiritualized. We are to work at the same time for both worlds. As Paul pictures it, we are not alone to get upon the Rock,

---

* Compare 2 Cor. ix. 9 with Ps. cxii. 9.

† Prov. xxxi. 26.

or to be saved barely and nakedly "so as by fire." We are to do more. We are to be building all that we can of the temple whose gold, silver, and precious stones shall shine out in all their celestial and eternal glory on that great day when the wood, hay, and stubble of mere earthly possessions shall be swallowed up in the "fervent heat."*

Augustine, in one of his sermons at the Numidian city of Hippo, beautifully represents this heavenly privilege. He says:† "In a certain way the Lord our God wishes us to be merchantmen. He makes an exchange with us. We give what abounds here, we receive what abounds there. It is just as many transact commercial traffic; they give goods in one country and receive something else in another to which they come. Thus, for example, a man says to his friend, 'Receive gold from me here and give me oil in Africa.' It is not a transportation, and yet there is a transportation. He gets what he desires. . . . We give earth, and we receive heaven. We give the temporal, and receive the eternal. We give things corruptible, and receive the immortal. Lastly, we give what God has bestowed; and receive God himself. Let us not then be slothful in such a commerce as this. Let us not continue poor."‡

* 1 Cor. iii. 11–15. 2 Pet. iii. 7–13.

† *Sermon* cxxvii., on 1 Tim. vi. 7–9.

‡ JOHN CALVIN, in his *Commentary* upon the rule in 1 *Cor.*, spiritualizes its meaning somewhat after the style of Augustine. He says, "To 'treasure' is to bury. The safest and best treasury is the bestowment of things to holy uses. . . . God submits to be a debtor to the poor, that he may return what we give to him, with ample interest. These words of Paul agree with those of Christ, 'Lay not up for yourselves treasure on earth,'" etc.

INDUCEMENT TO PERSONAL AND HOME EFFORTS.

This setting apart of money for the Lord is designed to induce Christians to engage in personal labors for the spiritual welfare of others, and for the spread of the gospel.

A man is to lay by him *at home*, as the original text means. Christian influence should begin at *home;* in one's own family. For no other human beings are we so responsible. None are so dear. None, if we are what we should be, are so impressible by our influence. It was a joyful thing for Rahab, when she had gathered her kindred into her house, and hung the scarlet line out of the window, to know that all were safe from the slaughter of the war without and from the burning of the doomed city. What then will be the joy of the parents of a saved family—*all* saved!—in the last judgment, and in the burning of the world!

A capital secret of success in guarding a home and family from evil is to train them to habits of active and constant beneficence and usefulness. Warmth and health are better promoted by vigorous exercise than by wrappings, and fires, and stimulating draughts.

The savings and the earnings of the children and the mother for some Christian end, how they make beautiful and fruitful the growing plants! "Home" is the chief and great sphere for the ·exercise of woman's peculiar power. A father and mother should lovingly teach their children, like the disciples of the early Christian Church, to "make their little box a treasury" of "the church in the house," and early form them to habits of regular and intelligent acts of charity and beneficence. This instruction of the children is

the chief hope for the adoption of a higher rule of beneficence in the entire Church.

"Every one," as the Divine Rule says, should lay by at
home in order to make home a centre from which to reach
other families; to originate personal efforts for the conversion of sinners. A package of tracts placed, as opportunity offers, in the hands of the impenitent—a gift of a suitable book to the inquirer, or to the afflicted one—a warm
garment to a poor child or adult—some judicious help toward restoring a poor fallen one—a timely gift to a poor student—a sum placed in the hands of pastor or deacons for
special objects—a remittance to help one of the organs of
the Church in its appointed work, in some trying emergency
—if the little sums of each private treasury, in tens of thousands of sympathizing and praying families, could be set
flowing for such uses, as the spirit of this Rule indicates, the
whole fabric of society would, in a little time, begin to feel
that a new power was moving and elevating it.

We should imitate the life on earth of JESUS CHRIST,
"the friend of sinners." We should go in person to convey our charities. "It is," says Guthrie, "less the amount
given than the way of giving it that sweetens the cup of
poverty and reconciles the pensioners of our bounty to their
lot. Those kind looks and tones which bespeak the feelings
of the heart, you cannot transmit with the goods or gold,
the meat or messages which you send through the medium
of servants or societies, or any second party whatever. As
far as possible, therefore, every one should be the almoner
of his own charities, and carry the sunbeams of his pres-

15

ence into the homes of the poor." . . . "Speak as *Christ*, had he been in our circumstances, would have spoken; feel as he would have felt; act as he would have acted."*

The profession of union to Christ gives to every "member" of his spiritual body not alone a place, but some office and duty to perform for the benefit of the whole. Time does not allow the illustration of this evident vital principle of the Christian life from the Scriptures, from the example of the Primitive Church, and from the lives of the converts from heathenism in our foreign mission fields. We may only cite an interesting extract from the "Catholic Epistle of Barnabas," one of the earliest Christian writings extant. Barnabas, or the writer of it, exhorts the believers in Christ to unceasing acts and labors of charity. He says:† "Call to remembrance, day and night, the future judgment. Thou shalt seek out every day the persons of the righteous, and both consider and go about to save others by the Word, and meditate how thou mayest save a soul. Thou shalt also labor with thy hands to give to the poor that thy sins may be forgiven thee. Thou shalt not hesitate whether thou shouldest give, nor having given murmur at it. Give to every one that asketh, so shalt thou know who is the good Rewarder of thy gifts."

The late admiral Foote was an example of one who made his calling a means of serving Christ. During a visit to Siam he was entertained at a royal dinner. On taking his seat at the table, he bent his head and asked a blessing upon the food and guests. The king was surprised, and remarked

---

* *Our Father's Business*, chap. iv.

† *Epistle*, sec. xiv.

that he had supposed such a custom belonged only to the missionaries. *"Every Christian is a missionary,"* replied the faithful admiral. The foreign missionary work has been greatly indebted to some naval officers, merchants and officers of government, who have acted upon the conviction that "every Christian is a missionary." Is it not as true of those who are at home? Has not every man and woman a mission field within reach, in which there are many of those which are lost to seek and save, for whom to spend and be spent?

CHAPTER XII.

THE SAFEGUARD OF RELIGIOUS AND CIVIL LIBERTY.

YOU hold in your hand a United States legal-tender note. Consider it minutely. There is stated upon it the Act of Congress which authorized it. You see no such paper or declaration from a heathen or Mohammedan government. This fastens our attention upon all the chain of history which preceded that Act, and shaped it, the growth of Christianity, our long struggles for civil liberty, the Magna Charta in the meadow at Runnymede, the bloody wars, the successive revolutions, the refuge and conflicts in a new world, the establishment of methods for securing the representation of the rights of every man in every law that is made, and in every dollar of tax that is laid upon his property and labor. All those centuries of Christian influences and development of civil rights are represented in that note. The pictures of the capitol and of historical scenes, the portraits of deceased presidents and statesmen, are designed to impress these remembrances.

To place that note in your hand, there were necessary meetings of the state legislatures to choose senators, and elections in every community for members of the house of representatives, who were to consult and authorize the issue; the consent of the President as chief of the executive department of the government; and systems of revenue with all their vast machinery of men, and property, and armed power, to provide means to make good the "promise to pay." Without all this authority and these provisions, these paper pledges would be worthless.

The payment is guarded by an immense array of checks and balances; by signatures of officers responsible to the government; by careful records of every series of issues and of every payment made; and by the placing of its proper number on each note of the millions that are put forth.

Acts of counterfeiting, or tampering with the note you hold, are prevented or punished by legal enactments; by a complicated judiciary system; by universal police agencies.

Expensive machinery, and the aid of numerous sciences and arts, are applied to make the note easily distinguishable, and secure from imitation.

It is by such reflections as these, upon forms or usages which are so common that it is only now and then we are led to remember that they are the fruit of a tree which has been eighteen centuries in ripening, and which is a graft from another tree which had been growing as much longer in Palestine, that we are brought to conceive and realize how sacred is the trust of money in the theory and organization of the State, how jealously it is guarded by the State on every side, and with what exceeding watchfulness every payment of it is regarded.

The final object is to secure perfectly the rights of the individual. It is to guard the proceeds of his labor. It is to fulfill the expression of his will as to how a reasonable share of those proceeds shall be applied for the maintenance of order and the punishment of crime.

How precious to us beyond description is the civil and religious liberty to which through so many generations of growth and conflict we have attained! What so important as to preserve it, to use it wisely, and to transmit it to our children! How necessary for the Church of Christ, which after so long a time has come to the enjoyment of this liberty, thoroughly to inform herself as to its meaning, and to fortify it by such methods as the Giver of all good has ordained, that it may not again be insidiously or wrongfully taken from us, or from those to come after us.

Let us trace, for a moment, the great sources of religious and civil liberty. This will prepare us to estimate aright the provision for its preservation which God has made in the Rule for Christian Giving.

THE THREE CHIEF SEATS OF RELIGIOUS AND CIVIL LIBERTY.

It is one of the extraordinary coincidences of history, which all are not of chance, that peculiar analogies to each other have existed in the origin and constitution of three nations which have been the chief seats of religious and civil freedom—Israel, Switzerland, and the United States of America.

Israel was a confederation of thirteen republics; the two sons of Joseph being constituted the heads of distinct tribes—though the tribe of Levi, performing the universal duties of priests, judges, and physicians, was only allotted forty-eight cities, which were distributed among the territories allotted to the other twelve tribes, and its sustenance was provided for by the offerings to the Lord.

The resemblance of the constitutions of Israel and Switzerland long ago attracted the notice of scholars. Professor Michaelis, of Gottingen, in the last century, said,* "The constitution of Israel may be considered as in some measure resembling that of Switzerland, where thirteen cantons, of which each has a government of its own and exercises the right of war, are all united into one great republic. All the twelve tribes had at least one common weal. They had general Diets, of which we find examples in the twenty-third and twenty-fourth chapters of Joshua. They were bound, at least by law and compact, to take the field against a common enemy." "The form of the republic established by Moses was democratic. Its head admitted of change as to the name and nature of his office, and we find that, at certain times, it could subsist without a general head." "Moses seems to have been very desirous that the nation of Israel should always preserve the constitution of a free republic," still he "allows the Israelites the choice of a king," but "specifies the limitations of his power," and "that they must never elect a foreigner."†

While this scholar was preparing for publication these observations, thirteen colonies in the wilderness of the New World, of which he took little thought, were holding their counsels preparatory to forming a republic now ten times greater than either of the two preceding, in the constitution of which most of the principles indicated are embodied, along with others which secure, we trust, permanent free-

* *Comment's on the Laws of Moses*, b. II., chap. vi. and vii., published in six volumes, in 1770–1775.

† Compare Deut. xvii. 14–20.

dom to its people in the state and in religion—a republic whose power, knowledge, and wealth we would fain hope will be consecrated to the God of Israel, and thus make it like Israel a light to all lands.

Now let us consider attentively the source of our free institutions, in the appointments which God made for the people of the Israelitish republic. We will find in those ordinances the germs of all our ideas and rights of this kind.

EDUCATION OF ISRAEL IN THE SPIRIT OF LIBERTY.

The original constitution of the Jewish theocracy was truly wonderful for that age and for that quarter of the world. Both the religious and civil elements of government fostered independence, freedom, and the dignity of the individual; and, at the same time, as the highest means of producing such a character, encouraged acts of direct approach to God, communion with him, and responsibility to him as Creator, Lord, and Final Judge. All worship of the Jews had to be voluntary, else it was not acceptable. God said to Moses, "Speak unto the children of Israel, that they bring me an offering; of every man that giveth it willingly with his heart ye shall take my offering." It was said that, without the spirit of personal respect, "he that killeth an ox is as if he slew a man : he that sacrificeth a lamb as if he cut off a dog's neck."*

In all acts of religious worship the people were taught the principle of equal rights, equal acceptance, and equal accountability, before God, whatsoever the earthly distinctions. "The rich and the poor meet together; the Lord is the

* Ex. xxv. 2. Isa. lxvi. 3.

maker of them all." Special concessions were made as to the animals, or quantities of the materials, to be offered in the sacrifices and oblations of the poor; and generous provisions for their relief and protection. But the equality of their personal relations to God was assured in such laws as that requiring of "every one" "an half shekel" as a special memorial unto the Lord "to make atonement for their souls;" "the rich shall not give more and the poor shall not give less than half a shekel." "Every male" in the nation must come, three times in the year, from whatever distance in the land his home might be, to render personal worship at the temple.

In numerous forms, direct vows, oblations of gratitude for particular mercies to self and the family, and acts of special covenant with God, were encouraged. "Either man or woman" was explicitly authorized "to separate themselves to vow a vow of a Nazarite unto the Lord." And the people were taught that the priestly tribe was but a substitute of convenience for the first-born son of every family. The final principle as to all God's people is: "Ye are a royal priesthood." Thus every institution of the old dispensation seems designed to teach them the dignity of their high calling.*

Forms of Presentation of Offerings.

One of the most efficient guarantees of religious and civil freedom to the Jew was one which delivered him from any interference of others in the choice and presentation of all

* Prov. xxii. 2. Ex. xxx. 15; xxiii. 17. Num. vi. 1-6. 1 Pet. ii. 9.

that he gave to purposes of worship and the maintenance of the priesthood and its related civil offices: he was always required to "*bring*" in person all his offerings. If sacrifices were to be made, it is said, a score of times, every man "shall *bring* them unto the LORD;" or he "shall *bring* them unto the door of the tabernacle of the congregation;" or he "shall *bring* them" "unto the priest."* If first fruits were offered, a singularly beautiful act was performed. The law said,† "Thou shalt take of all the fruits of the earth, which thou shalt bring of thy land that the LORD thy God giveth thee, and shalt put it in a basket, and shalt go unto the place which the Lord thy God shall choose to put his name there; and thou shalt go unto the priest that shall be in those days, and say unto him, 'I profess this day unto the LORD thy God, that I am come unto the country which the LORD sware unto our fathers for to give us;' and the priest shall take the basket out of thine hand, and set it down before the altar of the LORD thy God." Then the donor was required to recount God's great goodness in bringing the nation out of Egypt, and say: "and he hath brought us into this place and hath given us this land, even a land that floweth with milk and honey: and now behold I have brought the first fruits of the land which thou, O LORD, hast given me." And, he is instructed, "thou shalt set it before the LORD thy God, and worship before the LORD thy God."

When the Lord is angry with Israel for their negligence, what does he do? Rebuke the priests and Levites for not going about and gathering the fruits of the ground and

---

* Lev. ch. iv., v., vi., etc.　　　† Deut. xxvi. 1–11.

money due to his service? No! He rebukes the people for not themselves *bringing* them. "Bring ye all the tithes into the storehouse." In the days of great revival, when the nation is stirred with zeal for the building of the tabernacle, or the first or the second temple, the people "bring the offerings into the house of the Lord," so that there is abundance, and perhaps "a great store" is left.*

ORIENTAL TREASURIES.

In the large enclosures, and numerous edifices connected with a temple in the East, abundant provision is made for treasuries and depositories of various kinds in which money, valuable gifts made of gold, silver and other materials, and oblations of grain, clothing, and other articles of use, can be received and stored. So in the temple at Jerusalem, there were treasuries of gold, silver and "dedicated things," the pattern of which David, by Divine instruction, gave to Solomon. These arrangements were restored by Nehemiah in rebuilding the temple after the captivity.†

Some of the most interesting passages in the life of Christ are those pictures of him by the four evangelists which show him sitting in this part of the sacred enclosure, to instruct the people who came to bring their gifts, as to the true principles of religious beneficence.‡ The gifts of money were cast into chests with trumpet-shaped mouths.§ The

* Mal. iii. 10. 2 Chron. xxxi. 10.

† 1 Chron. xxviii. 12; xxvi. 20. Neh. xii. 44.

‡ Mark xii. 41–44. Matt. xxii. 15–22. John viii. 1–20. Mark xi. 12–19; and Matt. vi. 1–4.

§ 2 Kings xii. 4–15. Comp. JOSEPHUS, *Jewish Antiq.*, IX., viii. 2.

synagogue service, after which that of the New Testament Church was formed, required collections for religious uses to be made each Sabbath. Chests were provided near the door in which the money was dropped as worshipers passed in or out. The Christian Church continued this usage. Our Lord apparently indicated in the sermon on the mount the duty of guarding against ostentation in this act, which many did "to be seen of men" in that public place. The early Christian writers mention boxes, chests, treasuries, or depositories, by different names, according to their size and character.*

THE PERMANENT GUARANTY OF LIBERTY.

The Divine Head of the Church, in giving to his people an ordinance designed to be universal in all lands, wheresoever it shall be successively planted, and to be its guide for all time in so vital a matter as the collection of money for its support and dissemination, illustrated his omniscience by including in it the best human safeguard of religious and civil liberty. He makes it the duty of each individual "*himself*" to "treasure," or "put in the treasury"—that is, to bring and deposit, or contribute, in person—his weekly accumulations.

The illustrations of the meaning of this appointment which we have drawn from the former dispensation are so plain and full that not much more need be added here. All contributions must be made willingly. "Every man according as he purposeth in his heart, so let him give, not grudgingly or of necessity; for God loveth a cheerful giver."† The

* Such as θησαυρός, κἰβωτός, κἰβώτιον, γάζα, γαζοφῦλάκιον, *arca, gaza, thesaurus*, etc.   † 2 Cor. ix. 7.

gifts must be made in such amounts, at such times, and for such objects as each one chooses, subject only to such general arrangements as are required to facilitate them. There should be some means of designating their objects; which, with the present conveniences, may be easily done by using envelopes. It is a matter of choice whether the offerings be placed in suitable boxes at the door, or be collected by the deacons, or be laid upon a table at the close of the service. The former was the ordinary and for some reasons the preferable plan. The object is to cultivate the spirit of Christ's admonition, that the act be done, as its first end, with reference to our Father who seeth the secret purposes, and will give effect to them, and bless us, on earth and in heaven, openly; and that it be associated with the motives which are embodied in this Divine Rule.* Such gifts as are designed for the poor may be left in the hands of the minister and deacons to distribute, yet what is bestowed on the poor will come better from the giver himself.

But it is clear that undiscriminating general collections left to be divided, not according to the will of the giver, but the will of a church session, or according to proportionate allotments of a presbytery, synod, or general assembly, are not in the spirit of the Rule.

IMPORTANCE OF THIS GUARANTY.

It is of the first importance so to frame all the arrangements in relation to contributions of money in the Church as to maintain the principle of the ordinance that the individual shall himself "lay by him," and put into the treasuries,

* See more especially Part I., chap. iv., and Part II., chap. iii., etc.

and control the use of, the money which he gives to religious objects. And every financial scheme in the Church of Christ is fraught with danger which does not cultivate religious freedom, provide for intelligent acquaintance with all the objects and the agencies placed before us as channels for our benevolence, and promote an ever-increasing realization of our personal obligations to God and our final account to him.

It has been one of the distinguishing characteristics of the Calvinistic and Presbyterian bodies in Christ's Church, in all ages, to give great consideration to principles; and to resist the beginnings of those practices which other branches of Christianity have allowed to go on and obtain power, until they have been overwhelmed with the disastrous results. The lessons of the past with regard to the dangers connected with the collection of money are of special interest to us. The rights of the people cannot, in the light of them, be guarded with too much jealousy. How small the beginnings of the gigantic and tremendous corruptions of the Middle Ages! The pastors of rich churches became proud and assuming. Disparity of the ministry grew and became settled. Various orders and grades were created. The most powerful in the cities were denominated distinctively "bishops." Grand church edifices were erected, and lavishly adorned. Confiscated heathen temples were adapted to Christian worship, retaining their statues and symbols under Christian names. The ceremonies of worship became pompous and sensual. The Holy Spirit took his flight; religion became a thing of forms and ordinances. The revenues which had flowed in out of principles of grace and of missionary zeal were demanded by definite enactments of councils, and enforced by the arm of the civil ruler. The prostitution of the Church to the State, and, in turn, the lewd and imperious despotism of the Church over the State, and all the horrid impiety and debauchery of the Dark Ages, were the results.

REPUBLICANISM OF THE APOSTOLIC CHURCH.

The primitive church was republican, founded upon the thirteen apostles. There was a complete parity of its tribes, and a complete parity of its ministry. There was no principle more jealously guarded than that of the equality of its membership in the church, and before Jesus Christ its Lord. The rich man "with a gold ring and in goodly apparel" was not to be set higher, or his gifts esteemed more, than the "poor man in vile raiment," for with the "Lord Jesus Christ the Lord of glory" there is no "respect of persons."* Numerous proofs of this principle in the life and teaching of Christ, and in those of the apostles, rise at once in every mind instructed in the Scriptures. The fruits of the restoration of this faith and principle of church order are seen in all the history of the creed of John Calvin and John Knox, and of the colonization from the lands which held it to this continent, whose institutions took their shape and impress from its order, and their life from its spirit; for our Revolution was the successful struggle in a new field of republicanism in Church and State against monarchism in both.

EFFECT OF PRINCIPLE OF INDIVIDUALITY UPON SOCIETY.

The effect of the principle, which in this chapter and
* James v. 1–5.

others previous we have been tracing, upon society, is thus described by an eminent American political economist:*

"A quality by which man is distinguished from other animals is *individuality*. The greater the variety of employments, and the greater the demand for intellectual effort, the more dissimilar become the parts, and the more perfect becomes the whole. In every society there exists a vast amount of latent capacity waiting but the opportunity to show itself; and thus it is that in communities in which there is no diversity of employments, the intellectual power is to so great an extent wasted, producing no result. Life has been defined as being a mutual exchange of relations; where difference does not exist, exchanges cannot take place. The more perfect the organization of society the greater the variety of demands for the exercise of the physical and intellectual powers, and the higher will be the elevation of man as a whole."

"Next among these qualities is *responsibility* before his fellow-men and before his Creator for his actions. Responsibility grows with the growth of individuality. And with every step toward perfect individuality men learn more and more to appreciate their severe responsibility toward society at large and toward their Creator for the careful preparation of their children for the performance of their duties to both."

RELIGIOUS THE FOUNDATION OF CIVIL LIBERTY.

Religious liberty is the ground of that of the State. Without a solid foundation there, civil liberty cannot be comprehended, or established, or maintained. Of this we have most

* HENRY C. CAREY, *Principles of Social Science*, chap. ii.

sad illustrations in the vain efforts of Romanist nations to imitate our republican institutions.   The ablest statesmen aver this truth.   Mr. Webster says:* "To the free and universal reading of the Bible men were much indebted for right views of civil liberty. The Bible is a book of faith, a book of doctrine, a book of morals, and a book of religion, of special revelation from God ; but it is also a book which teaches man his own individual responsibility, his own dignity, and his equality with his fellow-man." '

The historian Bancroft vividly describes the powerful influence of Calvinism upon Europe in the Reformation. " It aroused every intelligence to acts of private judgment ; changed a dependent, recipient people into a reflecting, inquiring people; lifted each human being out of the castes of the Middle Ages, to endow him with individuality; and summoned man to stand forth as man." "Longing to introduce the reign of righteousness, it invited every man to read the Bible, and made itself dear to the common mind by teaching as a divine revelation the unity of the race and the natural equality of man."†

The wise Lieber‡ shows the very great dangers of the centralization of power, and the necessity of sufficient checks and balances to it: "Power, according to its inherent nature, goes on increasing, until checked.   Montesquieu says, 'It is a lasting experience that every man who has power is brought to the abuse of it. He goes on until he finds its limits.'   And it is so with 'every man,' because it lies in the very nature of power itself."

* *Works*, i., 102.   † *History of United States*, iv., 151–154.
‡ *Civil Liberty and Self Government*, I., 169.
16

CHAPTER XIII.

THE MEASURE OF CHRISTIAN GIVING.

WHAT do men think of the farmer who, coming into a heritage of many broad and fertile fields, greedily eats up the stores of wealth which have been accumulated, and stingily puts into the ground for future seed only handfuls where he should scatter bushels? What of the merchant who ruins a great commercial venture by dishonesty in light weights and short measures? What of the king going to make war against another king, who sends ten thousand to meet him that comes against him with twenty thousand, opposes men naked and hungry and unarmed against a well-appointed and disciplined army, and thus insanely and shamefully sacrifices the welfare of his people and kingdom? By such common and absolute necessities, and by men's instinctive condemnation of those who neglect the means by which they are to be provided for, we see illustrated the importance of the closing provision of the Divine Rule for Christian Giving—that is, that the advancement of religion in the world, being done through human instruments and common means, requires expenditures of labor and money proportionable to the ends in view. As our Lord Jesus says, we must sit down and count the cost, and adapt means with reference to their sufficiency for the designs. It is tempting God, rejecting his providential arrangements, and making all that behold it begin to mock, when that sufficiency is not weighed, and its requirements fully met. Christ says that those who do not count and pay the cost of his service cannot be his disciples.*

The *measure* of Christian giving is the subject of the last provision of the Divine Rule. It is one with which the earnest soul of the apostle is full. "O ye Corinthians!" he cries out beneath the painful burthen of it, "our mouth is open unto you; our heart is enlarged! Ye are not straitened in us, but ye are straitened in your own bowels."† Oh learn mercy and charity! "For ye know the grace of our Lord Jesus Christ, that though he was rich, yet for your sakes he became poor, that ye through his poverty might be rich." Do we not approve ourselves to be his ministers by our sacrifices for you—choosing to be poor, yet making many rich; having nothing, yet possessing all things; and seeking to inspire you with the same self-denial, and liberality, and zeal! "This I say, He which soweth sparingly shall reap also sparingly; and he which soweth bountifully shall reap also bountifully."‡

INTERPRETATION OF THE WORDS.

Paul concludes, by inspiration from God, the great rule for Christian giving by affixing a standard, or measure, for our government in performing this vital duty of the Christian life. He says it should be, in the words of our com-

---

* Luke xiv. 28-33.   † 2 Cor. vi. 11, 12.   ‡ 2 Cor. vi. 11, 12; viii. 9; ix. 6.

mon version, "as God hath prospered."* Hodge says: "literally, '*whatever has gone well with him.*' He was to lay aside what by his success in business he was able to give. This is another principle which the apostle would have Christians to act upon. Their contributions should be in proportion to their means." Alvord translates the words, "whatsoever he may by prosperity have acquired." Olshausen understands it, "as far as the circumstances of each sanction it." Scott says, "let every man treasure up a proportion of his gains according as God hath prospered him during the preceding week." Bloomfield, Poor, in Lange's Commentary, and others, give it precisely thus, "*according as*, or *in respect to whatever;*" the pronoun and adverb having a general and potential character; the verb being "literally, '*to be set forward on one's journey.*'"

When we trace out the form and uses of the Greek verb we find that it is in the *passive*, signifying *reception* of the prosperity, and thus "there is a tacit reference to the Almighty." The word is used in three other places in the New Testament, Rom. i. 10, and twice in 3 John, 2, where there is an allusion to verse 6. The one word in Rom. i. 10, is translated in full by five in our version: "*might have a prosperous journey.*" This is the figure, then, which the Divine Rule implies. We are like ancient Israel, traveling to a land of promise. Jehovah marches with us in the pillar of cloud and of fire. He guides us, and defends us, and supplies all our wants. He gives us bread from heaven to eat. "As it is written," says Paul, "he that had gathered much had nothing over, and he that had gathered little had no lack."

* ὅ τι ἂν εὐοδῶται.

Do "ye, having all sufficiency in all things, abound to every good work; as it is written, he has dispersed abroad; he hath given to the poor; his righteousness remaineth for ever."*

In the Septuagint Greek, which Christ and the apostles read and quoted, we find this same word used in another appropriate sense. It is said that David had prepared gold, silver, brass, iron, timber, stone, and all things needed; and had "set masons to hew wrought stones for the house of God," and laborers to do other preparatory work. But he had "been a man of war and had shed blood," a conqueror rather than a builder. So he gave it as his last charge to Solomon, his son, "Now, my son, *prosper* thou, and build the house of the Lord thy God, as he hath said of thee." And again, "Then shalt thou *prosper*, if thou takest heed to fulfill the statutes and judgments which the Lord charged Moses with concerning Israel."† There are several Greek words which mean to "prosper," but this particular one used by Paul is the same which is used in the Septuagint in giving David's charge, in both these passages. Such an illustration is one of the most natural and suitable within the range of the apostle's knowledge. Christ was a conqueror, though only by the shedding of his own precious blood; to those who became heirs of the blessings gained is the charge given to build. "Let every man 'bring' to be wrought into a fitting place in that temple, whatsoever he hath prospered in;" gold, silver, precious stones, brass, iron, stones, "*anything soever*" that the Lord has prospered him in. Every man has something that will be of use in a great

* 2 Cor. viii. 15; ix. 8, 9.

† 1 Chron. xxii. and xxix.; xxviii. 3, 11, 13.

building; the poor, the rich, men of every occupation or capacity, with any kind of prosperity, can find things which they may turn into gold and silver to give for it. Males and females, old and young, all can find some work that they can make profitable thus. There is no mechanical employment, no material gift, which cannot be put into a form to occupy some place in the construction of all the vast and varied parts of the edifice, which is to be reared through so many long centuries, and whose area is to be commensu-. rate with the habitable world.*

It is worthy of remark, that this same Greek word is again used in the Septuagint with regard to the repair of the temple by Hezekiah. He was the honored agent of a great reformation, or revival of religion. The book of Chronicles relates how he "*prospered* in all his works," save in the matter of the king of Babylon; how he revived the ancient law, so that "the tithe of all things they brought in abundantly:" how "the people and the strangers rejoiced," "so that there was great joy in Jerusalem, for since the time of Solomon the son of David king of Israel there was not the like in Jerusalem."

Paul seems likewise to resume in the sixteenth chapter the same illustration, which is so striking to an Eastern mind, from a previous use of it in the third chapter of this epistle. In that chapter he pictures Christ as the great rock on which a temple is founded; himself a minister of the gospel, like a master-builder; they the workmen under his direction. "But let every man take heed how he buildeth thereupon." He warns them to avoid collecting there combustible mate-

* Compare Part I., chap. ii.

rials, or putting up round about or within the enclosures of the edifice the huts of thatch which are so common in those warm climates, and which so often catch fire from the fagots with which the workmen cook their meals, and burn at once to ashes. There is a day coming, he says, when "the fire shall try every man's work of what sort it is." If it be incombustible, "gold, silver, precious stones," he shall receive a reward; if it be combustible and perishable, "wood, hay, stubble," he shall suffer loss. So there are men who shall be saved upon the rock, as it were by fire. They are rich here, but their property is not builded into the temple. Their lives have been so barely, hardly Christian, all they have done and earned has been so earthly, so selfish, that they shall suffer the loss of the whole. They shall stand in heaven among the lowest and last, inasmuch as they have so abused the trust of talents and means which might have made them among the first.

This is Christian doctrine. It is such as would be very effective when addressed to people converted from heathenism, in that it is one of the elementary principles of natural religion which are found in all systems of it, those of the present as well as those of the past. It is a principle which our much fuller and clearer light should make a guiding and influential one with Christians now.

The grammatical form of the verb in the Rule should be observed. The gifts are to be from what one "*hath* prospered in." The consecration is to be retrospective; from what things are already in our possession. It is not to be promissory. This provision of omniscient wisdom corrects one of the mistakes by which churches sometimes try to conquer the natural avarice of the human heart, and by which men defer their obligations to God, and cling a little longer to their money. It is to be ready for the calls of God's providence and the necessities of the church; "*that there be no gatherings when*" they "*come.*"

This important idea is constantly traced in the appointments of the old dispensation. The gifts of God in each season and of every kind were to be gratefully acknowledged by rendering the first-fruits, or oblations, when ripe; and the sacrifices of animals when they attained a certain age; or else by the payment of the redemption money then due for each. But God does not make demands of us upon the credit system. Paul says our liberality "is accepted according to that a man hath, and not according to that he hath not." It is a mere sop to covetousness for us to promise what we have that is already due, and thus withhold it for a time. It is presumption to promise for the future, when we know not what a day may bring forth. It is a crime against humanity to refuse what bread would feed some famishing souls to-day, because we hope to spare more easily next week, or next month, or to leave more after we are dead. The root of promissory notes and subscriptions is too often, alas! ostentation; love of the praise of men rather than that which cometh from God. The general principles of this New Testament ordinance are opposed to them. It is a great mistake, practically, for pastors to solicit from a people promises to pay so much a week, or quarter, or year, to a round of benevolent or ecclesiastical objects; and to appoint collectors to gather up the money. The plan is burthensome to some, hurtful to all; it lasts but for a time and is thrown away; it is a shift to avoid the neglect of the cultivation of the conscience of the people and the imparting of information and instruction which would make them give from principle. Nothing is gained by rejecting God's plan, which is the only wise one, that which in due time will produce by far the most abundant results, and that which he will accompany with blessings infinitely more valuable than silver and gold. "Give that ye *have*," "as God hath prospered."

THE DIVINE SEAL UPON PROPERTY.

"Ye are bought with a price," and so are "the Lord's freemen;" released from bondage to sin and hell, and so "thou owest unto me even thine own self."* All that men are and have they owe to be used as Christ's service demands. He may require "all" as from the apostles, when he needs the whole of one's life and time; or "all" in order to release one from the control of the world, as in the case of the young man who asked the way to inherit eternal life. A Zaccheus may give half his estate to some objects, and four-fold their claims to others. Christ certainly expects returns proportionable to men's means, five talents from those that have received five, ten talents from those that have received ten.

But there is needed some distinct seal of God's right in all our possessions: and there are required for the comfort and welfare of society some general and permanent regulations as to time and property. Such regulations are indispensable in the State and in secular concerns. They exist in every other system of religion on the face of the earth;

* 1 Cor. vii. 22, 23. Phil. 19.

in all forms of heathenism and Mohammedanism; in all
the ancient Christian churches, and in many of the modern.
All Christians without exception comply with the appointment of one-seventh of time for general sacred uses.   There
are some, however, who do not comply with that of one-
tenth as to property.   On what authority of God is it based,
and what is its nature under this dispensation?

INSTRUCTIONS OF THE LORD JESUS.

What does the King and Head of the Church say in regard to the form and measure of our common offerings?

In previous chapters* we have observed the general spirit
of his precepts.   They all tend to wise system, directed by
holy and loving principle.   Each servant in his place is to
be a "faithful and wise steward, whom his lord shall make
ruler over his household, to give them their portion of meat
in due season."   He reproves want of pecuniary forethought
and plans by the example of the unjust steward, which
shows how much wiser the children of this world are than
the children of light.†

On two occasions the Lord Jesus expressly considered the
measure in which money is to be contributed for religious
purposes.   On one of these occasions Christ makes a comparison between various formal observances.   A Pharisee,
with whom he was to dine, is surprised by his neglect of
ceremonial washings.   He replies: "Rather give alms of
such things as ye have, and behold all things are clean unto
you."   Our marginal translation reads, for "as ye have,"
"or, *as ye are able.*"   Such is the meaning of the original

* Part I., chap. iv., and Part II., chaps. i. to iv.   † Luke xii. 42; xvi. 8.

expression.* This contains the same idea with the Divine Rule given through Paul; "according as God hath prospered." Christ says, almsgiving makes "all things clean" to men; he makes conformity to the law as to giving money to be one chief outward evidence of real repentance and true piety, while he sets the ceremonial forms at naught, as no longer of any value; therefore, he says, "*give as ye are able.*"

On the other of the occasions referred to, Christ definitely says "*tithes*" "*ought to*" be paid; but that these offerings must be inspired by holy and spiritual motives. "Ye pay tithe of mint and anise and cummin, and have omitted the weightier matters of the law, judgment, mercy, and faith. These ought ye to have done, and not to leave the other undone."† Jacobus well explains this: "They paid tithes, even to the merest herbs, and were exact even to the smallest items." "It was not condemned. They did right to pay tithes to the utmost. But, with all their attention to the smallest matters, they neglected things of more importance, their social and religious duties;" and also the spirit from which all such offerings must be made. Their giving must be from holy principle, both as to the measure and as to the motives.

It was on the Wednesday previous to his crucifixion when he spake these words. Within sixty hours he was to die. The cross, the bloody atonement, the agony of the garden, the sepulchre, the resurrection, all were just before him, and in full view to his omniscient eye. What did he mean

---

* Luke xi. 43. τα ἐνοντα, from ἐνειμι, to be in, or among, to be possible, to have in one's power.   † Matt. xxiii. 23.

by this solemn admonition to the crowds about him in the temple? It was as if the Son of God said to them, and to those who should hear them in every language in which to the end of the world his gospel should be preached: "If the Jew, amidst the dark shadows of the twilight, is taught of God to be so devoted, so liberal, and to make the gathering of means to serve and honor him one regular and chief object in every employment of his hand, how much should you henceforth *exceed* him. How much should you exceed his measure in the devotion of your money and means; and how much should you exceed him in the spirit of willing obedience, enlightened thought, mercy for the perishing of mankind and faith in the covenants of promise, with which those shall be poured forth."

THE ORIGINAL APPOINTMENT OF OFFERINGS OF A TENTH TO GOD.

When we search for the origin of the appointment of a tenth for offerings to God, we soon discover the mistake of those who reject it as if one of those belonging to the ceremonial law, which was abrogated at the coming of Christ. We find that it existed before the giving of the law. We discover it five hundred years earlier in the days of Abraham, "the father of all them that believe, though they be not circumcised," who paid tithes to Melchizedec; and in the practice of "Israel," the type of all those that prevail in prayer, who promised them at Bethel. We go back further still to the earliest events in the history of the human family, before the deluge, and find the decimal system employed then in the appointments of God in regard to material things and ordinary time, parallel to that of sevens in regard to those of sacred time.

The system of ordinary enumeration by decimals is probably based on essential principles fixed by the Creator. Arithmeticians have asserted that a ratio of 16, of 12, of 8, of 4, or even of 2—which was proposed by Leibnitz—would in different respects be better than that of 10.   It has been earnestly urged that 8 is the best possible ratio, and its great superiority shown as a number susceptible of indefinite bi-section, and itself a cube (2^3) and whose square (64) is a cube (4^3), and as the best natural division in dry or liquid measures.   It has been confidently prophesied that, however prodigious the labor and expense involved in the universal substitution of this ratio of 8 for 10, it will be undertaken by some future age at a far greater sacrifice.   It has been asserted that we use decimals because man has 10 fingers and 10 toes.   But Sabbath is not kept on each seventh day because the knuckles of a man's hand have seven elevations and depressions which many persons find a convenience for remembering the days of the week, or the long and short months of the year.   Nor, if we choose to use 4 or 8 as a ratio, would it be because of the number of our fingers without the thumbs.   God has given to numbers the principles which govern them.   No nation, ancient or modern, except a few that have fallen into the most degraded ignorance, has used a ratio of any other number than 10 in its arithmetic. And each generation successively from the very beginning has found it *impossible to change what was handed down* to it, and was inseparably interwoven with all its history, religion, dates, measures and business.   Thus we are of necessity led to the conclusion that the ratio of *ten* was given to the very first members of the human family; that this method of computation was part of the inspiration of language from the Creator to Adam when he arrayed the animals before him and taught him to name them, and that the design apparently was in some way, like that of the seal of *seven* on time, to appoint it for religious ends in connection with property.

EVIDENCES FROM LITERATURE AND USAGES OF ALL NATIONS.

We may obtain many evidences from historical and other sources that offerings of at least a tenth to God was a primeval appointment, not for the Jews, but *for all nations.* This is as clear as, and the proofs are of the same character with, those which show that sacrifices were an original and universal type of Christ, or that the Sabbath was observed from the beginning and was designed for all whom God had created.

If we consider the principle at the foundation of each of the institutions referred to, it will appear evident that the same reason which would lead God to appoint a fixed and universal portion of *time* for his worship, instead of leaving mankind to observe any which might please them, would also require him to appoint a fixed and universal contribution of the *means* necessary for the maintenance of a priesthood and the' edifices and forms of worship. The means are manifestly just as necessary as the time. The religious offices of the priesthood must be regularly maintained. And it must be remembered that the costs of buildings, of education, teachers, books, and manuscripts, and often those of medical attention to the sick, of hospitality to travelers, and even of the settlement of personal difficulties, always have been and are now in the East mainly supplied from this fund under the care of the priesthood.

It is to be expected that if appointed in connection with the first institutions of religion, the decimal system must be universally prevalent in the world, and be traceable from the earliest history of its different nations.   And such is the case.   A multitude of instances may be gathered of religious offerings of one-tenth among all the ancient nations of the world.   As the priesthood were so largely the civil rulers, we see the taxes of various nations assuming this form, as in Egypt.   In time of threatened famine Joseph doubled this rate.*   This religious usage is traceable in the remotest nations, and exists among many of them at this day.   But our space does not permit illustrations to be given.   Another form of proof of the universal use of decimals, and their religious character, might be presented by selecting the words by which the first ten numbers are known in the languages of the principal nations in each continent, and in the island groups of the Pacific Ocean.   These words have often appropriate significations. Such a selection would exhibit also the geographical prevalence of the decimal system.   But our space does not permit the introduction of these tables; and besides we wish carefully to avoid all such supports for the duty in discussion as might tend to introduce here the dangerous religious formality of the Old World.   We may, however, present a

* Gen. xli. 34.

TABLE OF DECIMAL CHARACTERS.*

Arabic.	Possible Archetype.	Chinese Square.	Sanscrit.	Egyptian Hieratic.	Phœnician.	Assyrian Cuneiform.	Hindi.	Urdu.	Turkish.	Chinese Cursive.	Roman.
1											I
2											II
3											III
4											IV
5											V
6											VI
7											VII
8											VIII
9											IX
10											X
11											XI
12											XII
20											XX
21											XXI
100											C

* It is not necessary to note some interesting questions presented in connection with the forms in the following table. There are table of written characters, which have this advantage, that some of them are taken from architectural remains in Babylon, Egypt, and India, which have existed for thousands of years. The forms here given have been collected from the best original sources.

A FUNDAMENTAL MAXIM AS TO LEVITICAL TYPES.

Before we consider the teachings of the Levitical dispensation, in regard to the consecration of property, let us lay down a fundamental maxim which will help to make them more plain to the understanding. It is this, that in the whole system of types and precepts we may expect to find a parallel maintained between what relates to the offices of Christ and what relates to those of his Church and his people. If the sacrificial lamb represented Christ, the believer must lay his hands upon its head when it is to be slain. The mercy-seat where he answered requests was erected over the ark, but within the ark were laid up the stone tables of the law, which taught duty. Israel was "a chosen nation," but only while it continued to be "an holy nation." So in the symbols of Christ. Believers are elect, but it is unto obedience. If he is the vine, they must be living branches

Chaldean legends which say that the original archetypal numbers, whatever they were, were preserved upon bricks and stone when the deluge destroyed all the human race except the family of Noah— who is named in them Xisithrus. See remains of *Berossus* in CORY, *Ancient Fragments*. The only point of present interest is the evident unity of the source of the decimal system, far separated and widely different as were some of the nations whence these illustrations were drawn.

17

and bear much fruit, else they will be cast forth and burned. If he is the head, they must be members each having his own office. The cross of Christ is made the power of God unto salvation, and the same power works in them mightily. His suffering becomes the grand motive for their holiness and zeal. If he died for them and rose again, they must live as those that are •alive from the dead, and cousecrate their all to glorifying his name and to spreading with the spirit of heavenly messengers the glad tidings of his grace to men. Hence we conclude that if we find much minutely prefigured in the law of Moses in regard to the particulars of Christ's ministry, crucifixion, and the gifts of his Spirit, we may as plainly expect to see much in it as to the particulars of the believer's duty to the Church, and to a world which is all to be made subject to Christ. This obvious principle lies at the root of the question of the design of the Levitical appointments as to tithes. It was to be supposed that as the rudiments of the principle of proportionate giving are seen in the patriarchal period, now in that of the law they will be expanded and made clear, minute, and practical, to the end that the servants of God may clearly comprehend the nature and measure of their obligations to him. If this be plain let us proceed to examine the character and object of the tithes of the old dispensation.*

TITHE-PAYING IN ISRAEL.

And, first, a tenth of the produce of his employment was required of every man, even including the Levites themselves. "Behold I have given the children of Levi *all the tenth in*

* See Part I., chaps. iii. and iv., and Part II., chaps. i. and ii.

Israel for an inheritance, *for their service* which they serve, even the service of the tabernacle of the congregation." This revenue was devoted to the support of the tribe of Levi, as an equivalent for their relinquishment of their share in the territory and general possessions of the nation, as a salary in virtue of their office, for religious uses, and for offices of charity toward widows, orphans, strangers, and the poor. This tithe extended to the most minute sources of revenue, even to the "mint, anise, and cummin" of their vegetable gardens, and oil, wood, honey, vessels and other articles of manufacture or merchandise were included in it.* For the reception of these vast accumulations a portion of the temple grounds was devoted to storehouses and treasuries; and the same provisions were made in "all the cities," only the "tithe of the tithes" being brought up to Jerusalem for the use of the priests engaged in service at the temple. This principal tithe might be commuted by paying the value of an article with one-fifth additional. To receive, register, and distribute this property, and the money paid on various accounts into the treasury, a special body of Levitical officers was appointed. And upon it the priesthood, Levites, and their families, were primarily dependent for their living, in connection with the firstlings of the animals and also certain parts of the sacrifices.

A second tenth was annually required of the people for a different purpose. It was to be applied to charitable purposes, festivals, and family rejoicings, and matters connected

* Lev. xxvii. 30–33. Num. xviii. 20–24. 2 Chron. xxxi. 5–19. Neh. xiii. 5–13, 31; xii. 44; x. 38. Matt. xxiii. Luke xi. Rom. vii. 4.

with the three great annual feasts at Jerusalem; so that it was easy to be borne. Thus it appears that the first tithe only was of the nature of a tax.*

Every third year each man was required solemnly to declare before the Lord that he had been honest in the dedication of these two kinds of tithes to the uses appointed in the law.†

Spirit of the Jewish Contributions.

A thorough study of the financial appointments of the laws of Moses removes various misapprehensions of their nature which are prevalent among Christians. Some of the other laws were designed to prevent intercourse with Gentile nations, or for special ends, and were burdensome; and the Pharisees made others still to be a yoke which was hard to bear by their minute and severe interpretations of them. But we ascertain from these laws and from the history of the Jews, as compared with other nations, that these financial regulations were easy and beneficent.

The payments were entirely voluntary. They are supposed by most persons now to have been compulsory. This was not the case. Wines says,‡ "The rendition of the tithes was left entirely to the conscience and the loyalty of each individual Israelite. No compulsory process could be instituted to compel a payment of them, neither did the priests or the magistrates have any superintendence or oversight of the matter. It will readily be imagined that the law must have been often but partially complied with, and

---

* Deut. xii. 17–19; xiv. 22–29.   † Deut. xxvi. 12–15.

‡ *Commentaries on Laws of Ancient Hebrews*, b. II., c. viii.

sometimes wholly eluded.   That this was actually the case, appears from commands issued by the kings, such as that of Hezekiah, and from the censures addressed by the prophets to the Hebrew people.''*   This appears also from the spiritual blessings and curses pronounced in the law itself.

The summary of the law which has just been given shows that its appointments were most charitable in their nature. Its influence is seen among the Jewish people until the present day.   Those persons who visit .our public almshouses, hospitals, and charitable institutions, can bear testimony that they find in them no Jews, unless it may be some in places where there are none of their own people to help them.

The joyful character of the festivals, family gatherings, and public worship, which were supported by the pecuniary contributions, made that ancient religion, when observed in the spirit of its appointments by God, inspiring and happy beyond any that has ever existed, in any other land, or in any late age.   This is seen in the historical accounts of the enrapturing influence of the temple services,† but especially in the psalms appointed for public worship, which are chiefly in the latter half of the book.

This financial system reached every family and every individual.   It combined the interest and co-operation of the whole people.

It adapted the measure of contribution to the means of each one.   It sought something from each one; but made the amount to be given proportionable to wealth or income,

* 2 Chron. xxxi. 4.   Jer. viii. 10.   Mal. iii. 8.

† See Neh. viii.   1 Kings viiI. 66.   2 Chron. xxx. 21–27.

illustrating the New Testament rule, "according as God hath prospered."

We have but to compare this with any contemporaneous or later system of taxation: we have but to contrast the happy condition of the Hebrew common people with that of the wretched, vicious, savage condition of the poor in Rome, or in any ancient nation, and we must be satisfied that this is God's plan, a plan originating in infinite wisdom and infinite goodness.*

INTERPRETATION BY HEATHEN CONVERTS.

Can the reader whose eye falls on this passage so transport himself to the circumstances in which the first converts from heathenism were placed as to conceive of the interpretation which *they* would give to the Divine Rule and to the Old Testament light upon *the measure* of their gifts? How did the Roman, the Corinthian, the Macedonian converts understand the words "according as God hath prospered"? They had been brought up, as the heathen in India and China are now, to make daily and liberal offerings, oblations, donations, to scores of deities, in order to propitiate their care over the various apartments of the house; over the employments of each member of the family; over matters of private or public concern, the street, the city, the various elements; over birth, marriage, death, and the judgment after death. Thus their religion was to them a source of varied, perpetual, and large outlays. Their worship as Christians was often interrupted by the drums and flutes and noise of idol processions. Their streets were

* See on this subject also Part I., chap. iv., and Part II., chap. i.

thronged with frenzied devotees. Their eyes were pained with the costly expenditures of idol worshipers and temple services. Their lives were daily threatened. Their hearts were sickened by the atmosphere of horrible iniquity. Their homes were often agonized and made miserable by the domestic trials resulting from their rejection of beliefs to which many loved ones fondly clung. They saw the world lying before them all in sin and under the power of hell. Ah! how could *they* do else than spend daily of their means in acts of Christian pity and mercy, and put into the treasury of the church, which was to furnish and send forth laborers to resist and overcome the abounding iniquity, "whatsoever" their blessed Lord had "prospered them in," and enabled them without real suffering to give? A tenth would seem to their burning hearts a small proportion indeed.

Such was the spirit of the first believers in Christ. It was the glorious, and what appears to the nominal Christians of most subsequent generations the surprising, characteristic of those on whom the Holy Spirit fell with the power of its first descent. An exposition of the highest meaning of the Rule for Christian Giving is seen in the recorded practice of the converts after Pentecost. To such an extent did their joy in Christ, their confidence in his unlimited providence, their deep love to each other, and their ardent zeal for the spread of the glad tidings of salvation carry them, that they held themselves to be like brothers in the possession of a joint inheritance and engaged in a like work. "And all that believed were together, and had all things common, and sold their possessions and goods and parted them to all men, as every man had need."

Such, truly, also will be the spirit of the Church when the power of the Holy Ghost shall again fill the souls of men.

SPIRIT AND METHODS OF THE PRIMITIVE CHURCH.

When the first overwhelming torrents of the Pentecostal influences had settled somewhat into regular channels, we discover a tendency to conform contributions of money to methodical arrangements, and thus to equalize, facilitate, and maintain them.   The payment of voluntary tithes to the church became the general custom within one or two centuries after the apostles.   It was four centuries later before it was made compulsory by the synods.   To save extended quotations let us group together some brief passages from the Homilies of Chrysostom.

The preacher strikingly presents the lofty spirit of Christian liberality which is suggested by those words of Paul that immediately precede the Divine Rule, "forasmuch as ye know that your labor is not in vain in the Lord."   He exclaims, "What sayest thou? 'Labor' again? Yes! But labor followed by crowns, and those crowns above the heavens.   The primeval labor, appointed on man's expulsion from paradise, was the punishment of his transgressions; but *this* is the ground of the rewards which are to come. So that it cannot really be styled 'labor,' if considered both on this account and on account of the great help which it receives from above; this is the cause of Paul's adding the words 'in the Lord.'   For the purpose of the former labor was that we might suffer punishment; but of this that we might obtain the good things to come."

He guardedly and wisely suggests the measure of liberality: "What is much and what is little God defines, not by the sum of that which is given, but by the capability of the substance of him that giveth." "Let the laboring man, as for instance the sandal- (or shoe-) maker, or the leather-dealer, or the brass-founder, or any other mechanic, when he sells any article of his trade, give the first fruits of its price unto God. Let him cast in a small portion here, and assign something to God out of his profits, even though they appear somewhat small." " I speak not to lay down a law, nor to forbid the bestowment of more, but to recommend the contribution of not less than a tenth part."

QUALIFICATIONS OF PROPORTIONATE GIVING.

It will probably make the duty of the proportionate giving which is taught in the Divine Rule plain to every one and show how reasonable it is, how adapted to Christians of all classes and in all circumstances, and how efficient for its ends, if we recall some of the lessons of previous chapters and add the following explanation of the conditions which qualify it:

It is based on love to God and entire consecration to him in all things; and is associated with his worship.

It supposes that every one makes it his *business* to serve God in his worldly employments, whatever they may be, and to devote a share of their income or profits to the objects of his gospel.

A general proportion of this income is fixed upon, below which the giver will not go, except in extraordinary circumstances. He will continually try to advance it and will increase his rate "according as God prospers him."

This measure is but a "standard" of aim and effort for the personal convenience of the giver, and its arrangements and acts are voluntary with him.

The ordinary rate should, if possible, be not below one-tenth.

The standard should vary with the changing circumstances of men or women.

The Rule, with the subsequent remark and the interpretations in the next epistle, shows, that the private deposits and accounts of individuals and families should be weekly, *or when the money is received;* but that gifts and appropriations of it to various objects should be *when suitable opportunities* "*come.*"

The general rate should not interfere with special and extraordinary gifts.

Neither the rule as to the rate, nor the collection of the proceeds, must ever be made compulsory by enactments or processes of Church or of State.

The Church courts should manage the general agencies of evangelism and charity; should require opportunities to be afforded in every congregation for every one to give freely, and the communication of instruction and incitements necessary for weekly or frequent offerings; and should exercise discipline in cases of persistent omission of the duty to make such offerings to God and for his service, as for neglect of other Christian obligations.

These offerings must not be made a ground of ostentation, of supposed merit before God, or of reliance upon aught but the free grace of Christ and his atonement on the cross for salvation and eternal life.

Special Vows and Gifts.

A considerable gift came into the treasury of the Board of Education recently which was a thank offering from a lady for the conversion of her husband. Some other gifts have come to it from beds of sickness, or scenes of affliction. A gentleman educates two students for the ministry, year by year, in the place of two sons whom he had consecrated to it, but whom it pleased God to take from him.

Neither the Old nor the New Testament would be fairly represented did we not hold up its provision for special vows and gifts, as expressions of gratitude for extraordinary or peculiar mercies from God, or as the seals of covenants of greater devotion to him. This is a subject with which Christians of this day, and especially in this part of the world, have not made themselves acquainted, and the duties of which they have not practiced. Even our translation of the Scriptures is defective in rendering the words which relate to it.* We denominate our prayers "devotion," though we neglect entirely the *votive* part of them. Special gifts are calculated to kindle joyful emotions, and to lift

---

* Thus in the following passages in the New Testament, where the words εὔχομαι and εὐχή occur: Rom. ix. 3, "I *could wish ;*" 2 Cor. xiii. 9, "This also we *wish ;*" Acts xxviii. 29, "They *wished for* the day ;" Acts xxvi. 29, "I *would* to God ;" James v. 15, 16, "The *prayer* of faith ;" "*Pray* for one another." The same words often occur in the Septuagint; as in the *vows* of Jacob, Gen. xxviii. 20 ; Hannah, 1 Sam. i. 11; the shipmen, Jonah i. 16; and "to the Lord for all his benefits." Ps. cxvi. 12-18.

the soul to a higher communion with God.*   They are appropriate upon numerous occasions, "*according as God hath prospered.*"   We may instance the following:

In thanksgiving for temporal benefits; bounties of the year; successes in business; providential blessings.

In gratitude for spiritual mercies; conversion of self or of kindred; answers to special prayer.

To commemorate remarkable deliverances; restoration from sickness; preservation of life or property.

Occasions of family rejoicing; joint gifts from the members of it.

With seasons of special devotion, fasting, seeking a revival of religion, and manifestations of God's grace; for special wants or emergencies of the work of Christ.

To celebrate memorable events in a congregation; outpourings of God's Spirit; interesting events in the history of a church: ecclesiastical and religious meetings.

To praise God for civil and national blessings; to commemorate occasions of public interest, and acknowledge God as the author of all our political and social privileges.

With great appointments for prayer for conversion of the world, or for the educated youth of this generation, or for the instrumentalities by which the earth is to be brought to the knowledge of its Lord and God.

On all such occasions as these, special gifts are eminently suitable and pleasing to God.   He blesses them "an hundred fold" to those who bestow them.   If considerable, they mark eras of advancement to higher religious life, and more abundant spiritual prosperity.

* Compare Part II., chap. iv.

CHAPTER XIV.

THE HOMAGE DUE THE KING.

WITH the exposition of the Divine Rule for Giving, and principles embodied in it, the purpose of this book is accomplished. The various pleas for Christian evangelization, and the specific uses of the money given, are not within its scope. It only remains to declare, in a few concluding words, the conviction, which must be shared by those who have considered the facts and principles related to this subject, that we have reached a juncture in the great movements of the Divine government, when God can no longer tolerate our past careless, fitful, heartless, and unprofitable way of giving money for the communication to our dying and yet ignorant fellow-men of the knowledge of eternal salvation or eternal damnation by the divine Son.

THE DEMAND OF HOMAGE.

This is a coronation day! It is that final "acceptable time," and glorious "day of salvation," when the Father seems to proclaim, "I have set my King upon my holy hill of Zion," and to say to the Son, "Ask of me, and I shall give thee the heathen for thine inheritance, and the uttermost parts of the earth for thy possession."* It is re-

* See Psalm ii.; cii. 13–18. Compare Luke iii. 4–6. 2 Cor. vi. 2.

quired in monarchical countries, when an heir takes possession of a throne, and a new reign begins, that each vassal
shall come and bring tokens of his allegiance and support.
He kneels before the king or lord, kisses his hand, and presents him with appropriate gifts.   It was so in Israel,* and
so it is everywhere to-day.   The old English law required the
expression of *homage*† from a vassal by his kneeling ungirt
and with uncovered head before his lord, and saying, " I become *your man*, from this day forward, of life, and.limb, and
earthly worship, and unto you shall be true and faithful;"
and then the lord kissed him, or he kissed the lord's hand.
This act and kiss, and the accompanying gifts, were the sign
and seal of a mutual covenant.   The refusal of " homage "
by a vassal was the sign of rebellion.   It brought forfeiture
of lands, and home, and protection; and outlawry, and destruction.   The long delayed fulfilment of the covenant of
the Godhead is now apparently at hand.   In the stupendous warfare of this century, and by novel and mighty engines of destruction on the land and on the sea, the Great
Conqueror is breaking the power of his enemies literally, as
well as figuratively, " with a rod of iron, and dashing them
in pieces as a potter's vessel."   Empire after empire, kingdom after kingdom has been suddenly, violently, completely
crushed; it has been done by nations which are carrying in
their hands his written law.   Great systems of superstition
and sin, of human bondage and wrong, have been smitten
to the earth almost in an hour.   And so has it been with

---

* Compare Gen. xli. 40, *marginal translation,* and 1 Sam. x. 1.

† From the French *homme,* Latin *homo,* a man.   COKE *upon* LIT-
TLETON; *Institutes,* P. I., b. ii.

families and with men who would not "*be instructed*" by that law. To the reader, to every unmindful or rebellious person the voice, as of a trumpet, sounds clear and loud and near at hand : " Kiss the Son, lest he be angry, and ye perish from the way, when his wrath is kindled but a little." "Let all that be round about him bring presents unto him that ought to be feared."*

Propriety of the Demand.

The propriety of the demand for this homage from our glorious King, was the theme of our opening chapters; it has been our chief theme in the volume; and it is our closing theme.

What terrible woes has the love of *mammon*, and the disobedience to the royal claims of the Lord Jesus Christ, hitherto inflicted upon the souls of men, upon families, upon the Church, and upon the nations of the world!

What vast, universal, joyful, and everlasting blessings will descend from heaven, to restore and beautify the earth, and make it all a new " garden of God," when the full allegiance and gifts of man shall be rendered again to his Lord!

How much in accordance with the principles of justice, right, wisdom, and beneficence, in human systems, are those of the Rule of Christian Economy which God has taught the Church.   Of what infinite moment is the practice of it!

The Office of Christian America.

With what power and what wealth has God endowed this nation.   There live men who were born before this govern-

* Ps. ii. 12; lxxvi. 11.

272 GOD'S RULE FOR CHRISTIAN GIVING.

ment was born; and when its people were very few, and poor, and despised. Already it is one of the richest, most populous, and most powerful in the world.

It is a fact of indescribable magnitude and interest that America is a new hemisphere; and that Christianity is starting here as it were afresh from the hands of Christ and the apostles. She is stripped of all the encumbrances and defilements of the Old World. God reserved this great and wondrously rich and beautiful continent for the final exhibition of her heavenly spirit and power. The nations of the world stand gazing with admiration, and learning the simple lessons of spiritual truth which from the lips of her Lord she repeats to their listening ears. It is our part to array her in "the beauties of holiness," and put in her hand the sceptre of his strength; to personify in her the pure, lovely, and beneficent religion which shone eighteen hundred years ago.

To America it is given to renew once more among men the influences of the pure primal Church. Her place it is to evoke again from heaven the rushing mighty winds of the Spirit, which shall now swell and sweep around the world, and finally disperse its clouds of pestilence and gloom; to send her sons and daughters, with tongues of fire, as witnesses of the kingdom of the Lord Jesus, to the uttermost part of the earth. Oh, that she may have grace to bring and lay her boundless riches at his feet!